BE
HAPPY
YOU
ARE
LOVED

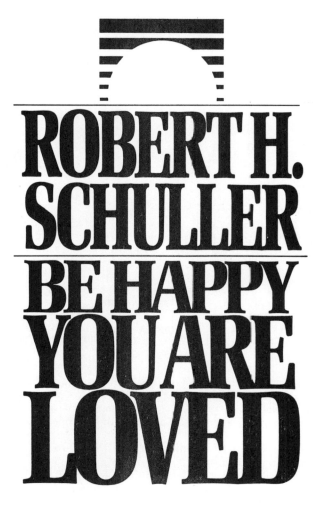

ROBERT H. SCHULLER

BE HAPPY YOU ARE LOVED

Thomas Nelson Publishers
Nashville • Camden • New York

Published in Nashville, Tennessee, by Thomas Nelson, Inc., and distributed in Canada by Lawson Falle, Ltd., Cambridge, Ontario.

Unless otherwise indicated, Scripture quotations are from THE NEW KING JAMES VERSION of the Bible. Copyright © 1979, 1980, 1982 Thomas Nelson, Inc., Publishers.

Scripture quotations from 1 Corinthians 13 in Part Two are from the Revised Standard Version of the Bible, copyrighted 1946, 1952, © 1971, 1973.
Scripture quotations marked TLB are taken from *The Living Bible* (Wheaton, Ill.: Tyndale House Publishers, 1971) and are used by permission.

Excerpts from Robert H. Schuller, *Self Love* (New York: Hawthorn Books, 1969), appear on pages 45–46.
Excerpts from Robert H. Schuller, *You Can Become the Person You Want to Be* (New York: Hawthorn Books, 1973), appear on pages 23–24, 114–119, and 139–148.
The prayer entitled "Faith," which appears on page 157, originally appeared in Robert H. Schuller, *Positive Prayers for Power-Filled Living* (New York: Hawthorn, 1976).

Printed in the United States of America.

ISBN 0-8407-5517-1

To Arvella Schuller,
my first wife and still
my wife today who more
than anyone else I
know lives a life
that reflects the best
that's in this book
and makes it easy
for me to believe
"God is love"

CONTENTS

Thanks to my wife, Arvella,
and my daughter, Sheila,
for their many hours of
work collecting, editing,
and correcting my work.

God
Loves
You . . .

You shall love the LORD *your God with all your heart, with all your soul, and with all your mind. . . . You shall love your neighbor as yourself.*

—*Matthew 22:37, 39*

LIFE: A JOURNEY OF JOY— IT'S POSSIBLE!

*Discover God Loves You . . .
And So Do I*

The call came late in the evening. John Wayne was facing surgery the next morning. It could be serious. He asked me to come and pray with him. I had met him socially on more than one occasion, but now "the Duke" wanted my prayers as a pastor and friend. He was fighting a recurring battle with cancer.

As I drove alone the next morning through the early darkness, I mentally checked through all the possibilities and prayed, "Dear God, what should I say to him? What can I tell him? Ask him? What prayer shall I pray with him?"

After the twenty-minute drive I arrived at Hoag Hospital in nearby Newport Beach. His room was well guarded. I was told to wait at the door. From inside the voice that all of America loves boomed out, "Let 'im in!"

I walked in and was greeted by his familiar grin. It was strange to see the man who personified the words *tough—true grit—* lying in a hospital bed, so strong and yet so vulnerable.

He lifted a long arm and stretched open his palm to slap and grasp my hand warmly. We talked frankly about his condition. As I began to pray, I watched his face, wanting to see the sight of a soul drawing near to God. His face clearly displayed anxiety; I had seen that creased brow in many tense moments on the movie screen.

"Oh Lord, I believe that John Wayne knows who Jesus is," I prayed. "Deep down in his heart he respects, admires, and loves

Jesus." At that point his face was transformed! The anxiety and tension faded, and his expression became as soft and gentle, tender, kind, and peaceful as the face of a child asleep in his crib! It was the most amazing sight! "And now, Lord," I continued, "Duke is putting his life, his body and soul—his future—into the hands of his friend, Jesus!"

A sweet hint of a smile appeared! When his eyes opened to meet mine, a tear glistened in each. Once more up came that powerful right arm and hand to grasp my hand. Once more the booming voice reverberated through the hospital room, "Thanks, Reverend Bob. I'll be O.K. now!" The smile was wide. The joy—genuine! The happiness—real!

A few days later I received an autographed photo that hangs on my wall to this day. It is Duke Wayne in a cowboy hat. Inscribed are these words: "Keep putting in a good word for me, Bob, I need all the help I can get."

I had no idea how soon I, too, would need all the help I could get.

❦   ❦   ❦   ❦

It was horrible! I was in Korea. My thirteen-year-old daughter Carol was in Iowa. There had been an accident. "We're amputating her leg, Reverend Schuller," the doctor in the emergency room in Sioux City said. My wife, Arvella, and I rushed to Iowa. In a matter of days letters of support and comfort came. Telegrams. Prayers. We all needed them.

Later, Carol was transported by a private hospital jet from Sioux City to Orange, California. It was a painful trip. After we arrived there were more cards, more gifts. And in the pile, amongst letters and photos of celebrities—politicians, professional athletes, entertainers—was an autographed picture of John Wayne. His eyes twinkled under the well-worn cowboy hat and scrawled across the bottom was this simple but profound message: "Dear Carol—Be Happy! You Are Loved!—John Wayne."

I only had to look around that hospital room, overflowing with expressions of love, and then to look at the face of my daughter, who was reveling in all the attention, to see that Duke Wayne was absolutely right. Carol could be happy. She *was* loved! Her face was beaming! Yes, she was wounded! Yes, her stump was in traction! But she was happy in her hurt!

"Was she *really* happy?" you ask. "How can that be?"

Well, she was genuinely happy—according to my definition of happiness:

Happiness is *not* . . .

Hollow Hilarity,
Giddy Gaiety,
Loud Laughter,
Flippant Frivolity,
Shallow Smiles,
Frantic Fun,
or
Chemical Cheer!

But Happiness *is* . . .

Genuine Joy!
Enjoyable Enthusiasm!
Serene Self-esteem!
Tender Tears!
Lasting Love!
Affectionate Encouragement!
Healthy Hope!

Affirming Faith!
Perceiving Possibilities!

Yes, happiness *is* . . .

Having a hand to hold!
Finding a heart to heal!
Leaning into tomorrow with love!

And, so I can say with total integrity that:
John Wayne was happy, in spite of a terminal disease. Why?
Because he was loved!
Carol Schuller was happy, in spite of losing a limb. Why?
Because she was loved!
And the good news I have for you is—no matter what it is you
are facing, no matter what condition you are in, no matter who
or what you are—you *can* be happy. For you, *too*, are loved!

**Even If You Think You Have LOST EVERYTHING—
Someone, Somewhere, Needs Your Love!**

The other day I was in my office studying when the
telephone rang. Since it was late and the secretaries had gone
home, the call came straight into my office, which seldom
happens. But if there's one thing I can't ignore, it's a ringing
phone!
I picked up the handset and the operator said, "This is a long
distance, person-to-person call for Robert Schuller."
"Go ahead; I'll take it."
"No," the operator responded, "it's for Robert Schuller. Are
you Robert Schuller?"
"Yes."
The voice at the other end said, "You've got to be kidding!

Everybody said I would never get through to you! It's a miracle! Are you really Robert Schuller?"

"Well," I said, "do you know me?"

"I watch you on television," she reported. "And I've got a terrible problem. I'm about to lose everything that I have."

"Do you have a tumor on the brain?" I asked her.

"No."

"Well, you're not in danger of losing your eyesight, are you?"

"No, not that, but . . ."

"Do you have cancer? Do they have to operate?"

"No."

"Well," I said, "let's see, you've got your eyes, your hearing, your sanity, and you aren't facing a debilitating surgery. Are you able to walk or are you confined to a bed—stiff, rigid, and paralyzed?"

"No, I can walk."

"Well, then," I replied, "you can walk, you can talk, hear, see, and laugh. Why, you've got everything going for you. You've got faith, too. You must believe in God, and you must believe I will respond with love, or you wouldn't even be listening to me! Or at least you wouldn't have called me!"

"Yes," came a feeble reply over the sound of sniffling tears.

"Then you still have what is most important; you have a love connection, right now!" I assured her. "Now affirm out loud: 'I am loved!'" She moaned and mumbled pathetically, but the words did come out!

"Now, can you think of one other person whom you love? A child? A neighbor? A delivery person? A grocer? A relative? An old and lonely person in a rest home? Is there someone you know who is in a hospital? Is there someone you can think of who has had surgery this past month or year? Or lost a husband? A wife? A child? Is there someone who got married recently? Can you think of someone who had a birthday or is going to have a birthday? Take a piece of paper and pencil and make an inventory of 'My Love List.'" She didn't respond. "Please, do it now! I'll wait!"

"O.K.," she said weakly. I heard a piece of paper rustling. Some moments passed.

I had no idea how long I already had talked with that woman! All I knew was that she was in a state of emotional panic, on the edge of desperation! Oh, how I felt for her! What compassion I felt for this woman, who—though she was a stranger—seemed to be one of my dearest friends. Why did I feel so close to her? Why did I care? Where did my authentic compassion come from, for a person whose face I could not see and would probably never see?

"Now read your list to me," I said, finally. She began to read her love list, a litany of love! It was a nice, long list! "So you haven't lost everything—because you still have someone," I assured her. "Your voice sounds stronger now! You do feel better than when we first started talking, don't you?"

"Yes," she answered, "I really do." Her words were stronger.

I was impressed. "Now, will you do something for me?" I asked. She agreed, not knowing what she was being set up for. "I've got a problem," I said.

"You do? Can I help you, Dr. Schuller?"

"So many people need my love," I answered, "and I'm so far from them that I cannot touch them. I get so many letters from unhappy people; they need someone—they need *me*—to call on them, talk with them, hug them, encourage them, kiss them gently on the cheek, but I'm too far away! And there are too many of them!"

"That's really something, Dr. Schuller; you must feel overwhelmed," she said. I sensed the caring—for me—in her voice!

"Will you help me? Please! To pass my love and God's love on to those around you who are unhappy?"

"I'll try," she answered sincerely. "Yes! I really will!" she assured me.

"Thank you," I said. "Now let's pray: Thank you God that *we haven't lost everything, if we still have someone left who needs our love!* Amen."

"Amen," came her voice—strong again.

"You have not lost everything, my friend," I added, "as long as you still have the best job in the world—sharing love. In a world where there is so much hurt and heartache, it doesn't make sense for anybody to say 'nobody needs me.' Someone not far from you needs your tender touch, your simple smile, your holy hug today."

Even If You Have FAILED IN LOVE—Someone, Somewhere, Can Give You the Courage to Try Again!

Have you suffered the disgrace of a broken relationship? A broken marriage? Are you afraid to try again?

You are not alone! Somewhere, there is someone whose love can overpower your feelings of failure and fear and give you the courage to love again.

I had the joy of marrying the celebrated pianist Roger Williams to his lovely bride, Louise DeCarlo. They stood facing each other, after dating for over *eleven* years. My eyes filled with tears as they said the vows they had written for each other.

Louise: My darling, I love you more than life itself. I know how much time you spend on your music, and that's a lot of time spent away from me. But it's that quality time that we spend together that's most important to both of us. I could never think of living my life without you. I shall love you till the day I die. And if God wills, I shall love you even better after death.

Roger: My darling, you're my girl. And you'll always be my girl. Because yours is the love that I hoped and prayed for, for all these many years. And yet, when I finally found you I was afraid. I was afraid because my first marriage had failed. I was afraid because, most of all, I hate to fail. Only your love, only your patience, only your understanding helped to turn this loser into a winner again. There's so much to say I can't find the words, except for these—I love you. I love you with all my heart. And darling, I'll be true, so help me God."

Roger added, "I asked my good friend Andrew to sing his composition, 'Winner's Song,' because today, Louise, I've become a winner again!

You're beautiful as a rose can be,
You're living in the love of my heart,
You're family, you belong to me
And nothing's gonna keep us apart,
Oh, nothing's gonna keep us apart.

I don't know a better way for life to go on,
You have made a loser sing a winner's song.
It's the beauty of your love that makes me so strong
With a winner's song!

You knew that I was a helpless child
Who happened to be needing a friend.
But win or lose you were there to prove
Your love would make me win in the end,
Your love would make me win in the end.

I don't know a better way for life to go on,
You have made a loser sing a winner's song.
It's the beauty of your love that makes me so strong
With a winner's song!

—Andrew Culverwell*

Even If You Have FAILED IN LIFE—Someone, Somewhere, Cares!

Bankrupt? Facing a financial catastrophe? Lost the family farm? Such failure hurts, but the only people who never *trip* are those who never *try*! I have met people who have failed miserably, yet they have recovered a lost happiness!

Could any failure be worse, more shameful, than going to prison?

One day in a bookstore, where I was autographing books, I looked up into the happy face of a man in his forties, I guessed. He looked so excited, so enthusiastic.

"Your book and the television ministry have saved me from total despair," he said. I listened and looked deeply into the warm eyes that were misting. "Dr. Schuller, I was an awful failure. Let me just tell you. I am in jail—today! I've been there a long time. But . . ." he tilted his head, nodding at a tall stranger who stood silently behind him, guarding him . . . , "they let me come out to meet you and thank you! I love myself—anyway! I have found God and have decided to turn my scars into stars! I'm your missionary in prison; I've got lots of tough guys listening to you! They're getting saved too! I have another seven months to go. When I'm out I'm going to try to keep going back to do the missionary work! I'm so happy! Thank you! Got to go! Goodbye!" He waved and was gone.

Even If You Are RIDICULED AND REJECTED— Someone, Somewhere, Accepts You!

Some years ago I flew to the Orient on a mission for the United States Air Force. As I put my foot down on earth after the last nine-hour leg over the Pacific, the man who stepped forward to shake my hand was a black officer with an eagle on each shoulder. He smiled and said, "Dr. Schuller, I am Bill King."

Colonel King, who became my host in Okinawa, was one of the greatest human beings I had ever met. At the conclusion of those few days, when we were driving to the airport for my trip to Japan, I thanked him for his graciousness, his hospitality, and his kindness. He looked at me and said, "Dr. Schuller, I want you to know that we don't give you good treatment to impress you. We treat you well because you're a human being."

Then he stopped to allow a group of children to cross the street. After they had crossed, he said, "And there is only one way to treat people and that is *first class!*"

Bill King has known racial prejudice in his lifetime. He has been ridiculed and rejected on occasion—simply because of his color. Yet, he has had friends and loved ones who loved him for the beautiful human being he is. As a result he has chosen to treat people everywhere one way—*first class!*

Even If LIFE HAS BEEN UNFAIR to You—Someone, Somewhere, Needs You the Way You Are!

"I've been handed a bad deck of cards," a man once said to me, disfigured, deformed, and bitter!

"But that's no excuse for choosing to be miserable and un-happy," I chided him. I remembered Mary, whom I'd met not long before in an eastern city. I first had noticed her face. She was a gorgeous girl, with beautiful red hair and dark brown eyes. Her make-up and her hair were like a model's. She could have just stepped from a magazine cover. Then I lowered my eyes from her glamorous face to the wheelchair below. She was tiny, and I couldn't see any shoulders. Propped in the chair was a little body, covered by a small dress. There wasn't anything there to hug.

I knelt by her wheelchair and said, "Mary, you're so pretty," and kissed her on the cheek. "What do you do?"

She said to my astonishment, "Well, I have my master's degree; I have a very successful business. I have joined your Eagle's Club! I've watched you on TV for twelve years. I know all the slogans: *Who can count the apples in one seed? . . . Look at what you have left, never look at what you have lost. . . . There is no gain without pain. . . . It takes guts to leave the ruts!* Dr. Schuller, thank you!"

I was astounded, amazed! This courageous woman reminded me of Max Cleland. Max is a guy who got on the wrong end of a grenade in Vietnam. The explosion blew off an arm and both legs. Now he works from his wheelchair, with one arm. He could so easily have turned his face to the wall and his eyes to the ground and quit, but he didn't. Recently, I asked him, "Max, what are you up to these days?"

"Oh," he said, "I wish you could be in town tomorrow night; I'm having an *Alive party*."

"Alive party! What's that?"

"It's to celebrate my *alive* day. That's the day when I lost my arm and legs."

"You *celebrate* that day? Like a birthday?"

"Oh, yes! That's the day I should have been killed and I wasn't! God kept me alive. So, I celebrate my alive day."

Even If You Are POOR—Someone, Somewhere, Will Treasure You!

There is poverty in America, and some people are severely underprivileged. Many feel they are trapped, that there is no way out. Do you see yourself in this predicament? You are not alone! Others have been where you are—but they broke free!

Take, for example, Dr. Rodrigue Mortel, an Horatio Alger

Award winner. Dr. Mortel has the distinction today of being the only foreign-trained black medical doctor to head an academic department in one of our 127 American medical schools. He is university professor and chairman of the Department of Obstetrics and Gynecology at the Milton S. Hershey Medical Center in connection with the Pennsylvania State College of Medicine.

Dr. Mortel was born and raised in Saint Marc, a small town located near Port-au-Prince in Haiti. The town had no electricity. His home had no water, no sanitary facilities. His father, who had only a fourth-grade education, was a self-employed tailor earning $30 a *year*.

Dr. Mortel's mother could not write nor read, but she helped support the entire family with profits made by buying and reselling vegetables in open air markets, using either the train or the family donkey as transportation. Since there was no electricity, Rodrigue had to study by the light of a kerosene lamp.

When Rodrigue went to Port-au-Prince to attend college and medical school, he boarded in a home that had electricity. However, the house was so crowded that Rodrigue had to study under the street lights or in the quiet of the park during his medical school years.

Finally graduating from medical school, Dr. Mortel practiced for two years in rural Haiti and then decided to leave Haiti for postgraduate training in the United States.

After eight years of postgraduate training in America, he became an obstetrician and gynecologist and a specialist in female cancer.

He then entered academic life and devoted his entire professional life to teaching, to cancer research, and to care of women afflicted with this dreadful and deadly disease.

Dr. Mortel attributes his supersuccess today to the faith instilled in him in his early childhood. He always was aware of the persistent presence of God in his life, as well as the powerful impact of prayer.

Today, Dr. Mortel exports to Haiti medicine, hospital beds, x-ray equipment, and whatever else he can obtain in this country that will help his former countrymen.

You, too, can go anywhere from where you are.

Even If You Are TRAPPED—Someone, Somewhere, Can Liberate You with Love!

As a pastor for thirty-six years I've met and counseled with thousands of persons who felt trapped—in a bad marriage, in an unfulfilling job, in an unpleasant neighborhood, in a hospital bed.

Again and again I have watched their moods change from despair to joy when they allowed their attitudes to change from the negative to the positive!

"I may be a shut-in—but I'm not shut out!" a bedridden young man said to me. "I've got lots of friends." And he gestured to the telephone and to the mailbox outside his window.

Sometimes, when we least expect adverse circumstances, in a flashing instant an unexpected event drastically upsets our cozy routine. We are trapped!

But love can set us free! Captain John Testrake, whose TWA Flight 847 was hijacked out of Athens, found that "love memories" liberated him from fear and depression before he was set free by the hijackers.

You read the headlines! Beginning on June 14, 1985, 145 passengers and a crew of eight were held hostage for seventeen days. Captain John Testrake was the pilot of that flight, and he has been hailed as a hero for his role in that drama. He has said that at the moment the wild-eyed gunmen came bursting into the cabin, amazingly he wasn't afraid.

But when they landed in Beirut for refueling, there were snags in getting the fuel, and the hijackers came close to hysteria. At that moment, with a pistol at his neck and a grenade in his face, Captain Testrake reached out to Jesus Christ, to whom he had given his life many years before. He decided to trust Him completely.

As John Testrake said in *Guideposts* magazine:

There was nothing new about the faith that kept me steady that first day. It was a part of me, just as knowing how to fly a plane was a part of me, but it had grown stronger over the years with each crisis, each sadness. In 1955 my infant son, William, was killed in an auto accident that nearly killed me, too. In 1976 my first wife, Patricia, died of cancer. My faith was there during that long year I was a single father to my four children, Debra, 23, Alan, 19, Diane, 18, and John, 14, all the while flying regularly for TWA and all the while making sure that we stayed close to our church in the little town of Richmond, Missouri. And there in that same church one Sunday, standing among some new members, was Phyllis Hisler. It was as if God touched my shoulder and said, "John, I have brought her here for you."

We married, raising children from both our families. Then, my oldest son, Alan, age 27, died suddenly. Once more I leaned upon the Lord and He was there. Each time I seemed to grow closer to Him. Little wonder that during the hijacking of Flight 847 I knew for certain that God was with me and I with Him. *

The flight engineer on Flight 847 was Christian Zimmermann, an ordained Lutheran minister. Both Captain Testrake and Flight Engineer Zimmermann spent their time in captivity reading the Bible and sharing inspiration. And on Sundays these two brave men had worship services for themselves. John led the singing of hymns, and Christian gave sermons that spoke of hope, of joy, of love for God.

What does Captain Testrake remember of those traumatic days? As he said in the *Guideposts* article, "I remember the constant presence of Jesus. He kept me from being afraid. He comforted me. He gave me hope. He gave me freedom, though I was a captive. And He is with me still as I continue to fly for TWA."

Even If You Are GRIEF-STRICKEN—Someone, Somewhere, Can Fill the Void!

I'll never forget the day I was in the Holy Land with a study group. I called home to see if everything was all right, only to hear that one of the young fathers in our church, Bob Trueblood, had lost his wife and his three children in an automobile accident.

Pam and Bob had married in 1969. They spent fifteen beautiful years together and were blessed with two sons and a daughter. Their home was one of love. On October 22, 1984, Bob took Pam out to dinner to celebrate her thirty-sixth birthday. The next morning he kissed her and the children goodbye as he left for work. That was the last time he saw them.

He arrived home after working late. The phone was ringing. Pam had gone down to pick up the children from their gymnastics class, about a two-mile drive from their house. The person on the phone was the mother of one of the children whom Pam was to have picked up. They should have been home an hour earlier.

Bob got in his car and drove to look for them. He stopped at a police barricade where he learned that a young man, who was drunk and driving eighty miles an hour, had struck the car carrying his family. He was told that his wife, his oldest son Eric, and his daughter Kerry were dead at the scene. His youngest son Scotty was at a local hospital where they were trying to save him.

The police raced with Bob to the hospital, but by the time he got there, Scotty had also died. Bob told me later, "As far as I was concerned, my life was through. My whole life had been built around work, my family, and church; all the loves of my life were no longer here."

It was a difficult night, a difficult week. Bob shed many, many tears. But at the end of the funeral, he said,

I began to realize something. I had lost my entire family, but two thousand years ago my Heavenly Father had sent His entire family, in the form of Jesus Christ, down here to die on a cross and that was done on purpose. Now, Pam's death and the deaths of my children were certainly not on purpose, but God loved you and me enough so that two thousand years later, I could go to a funeral and realize that while I was there with the bodies of my family, they were in heaven with Jesus and they were fine. I don't know how I'd have made it through the week without that realization. I looked to God and I had a choice to make. I could either blame God for what happened, and shake my fist at Him. Or, I could fall into His open arms and allow Him to love me through it. And that's what I chose to do.

Pam and Bob had been members of a Sunday school class at the Crystal Cathedral, the Becomers, and there were many events going on at that time because of the approaching holiday season. Attending those activities helped Bob a lot. At one of the events Bob began to talk with a young woman named Diane Moyer, who had been recently widowed and had just moved from Ohio. She understood Bob's pain because a year before she had watched her husband die of cancer. Six months after Pam's accident, Diane and Bob were married. With her came her daughter, who had the same birthday as Bob's! And then, on May 1, 1986, a son, Robert Henry, was born.

Bob said, "The good Lord gave me a number of things to help me through the biggest hole I've ever been in in my life— certainly one I never hope to see again. He gave me the support of this church, the support of a Sunday school class, the support of cards and letters, but more than anything else, it was the internal security of knowing Jesus Christ."

Even If You Are DYING—Someone, Somewhere, Loves You Forever!

Steve Miller is a handsome, young, articulate member of the Crystal Cathedral. He also is winning over muscular dystrophy.

When he was in his mid-teens, an energetic and athletic young man, all of a sudden Steve started getting tired. Some of his coaches thought he was just lazy. But when they took him to a doctor, a battery of tests showed that he had myasthenia gravis.

Steve was told that he could not be as active as he used to be, that his life would change drastically. He was put on medication and told that he would at best regain just 70 percent of his strength, stamina, and endurance.

Steve followed the instructions, but then one day an idea popped into his head. "What would happen if I developed myself to the point where my 70 percent was equal to a normal person's 100 percent?"

So with his doctor's approval, Steve started to build himself back up physically, mentally, and spiritually. Then Steve encountered two young people with muscular dystrophy who affected him deeply.

He met the first one in a hospital in Arizona. He went to visit a friend one day and in the next bed was a girl lying flat on her back and hardly able to move. Not wanting to be unfriendly, Steve went over to say hello to her. On the nightstand next to her he noticed a prescription for the same medication that he was taking. Steve was curious about why she was lying there flat on her back. When he asked her, she replied, "Because I have myasthenia gravis and the doctors told me that this is where I need to be." She told him that she was taking twelve pills a day, which seemed like a lot except that Steve was taking thirty-six and he was up and around, still active.

The second of Steve's profound experiences came when he was a volunteer staff member at one of the summer muscular dystrophy camps. Steve told me later,

At those camps, the staff has to bed check the kids every night. Some of the more severe forms of the disease, such as Duchenne dystrophy, cause muscles to atrophy and turn to fat. People with this form cannot move, even in their sleep. Just as we are, they can be uncomfortable at night. We just roll over, but they can't. The camp staff tried to help these patients stay comfortable.

So, we would bed check the kids every hour. One morning at about four I went in to check on a young girl. She was obviously in trouble, laboring to breathe. You see people don't die of muscular dystrophy; they die of suffocation. She was really having problems, so I called for help. I set her up to get the weight off her chest. The whole time that I was holding her there, she kept apologizing for keeping me up so late.

Tough times never
last . . .
Tough people do!
****

Just remember—
God loves you . . .
And I do, too!

Then she said, "I know I'm gonna die. But that's O.K. I'm happy. I've had a great time."

You know, Dr. Schuller, she *was* happy! She just kept on saying, "I'm not afraid, I'm happy." And then she died while I was holding her.

That was tough on Steve. But he said,

I didn't know it at the time, but later on I realized what a valuable learning experience that was. On one hand I had met one girl in a hospital with my disease and she had given up on life. But the other girl with the same terrible disease kept on being happy until the very end. They both had a *choice* as to how they would react to their situation.

You see, Dr. Schuller, I believe we are responsible for our actions, but we're also responsible for our *attitudes*. Good things happen to us and bad things happen to us and we can choose how we want to react.

I asked him, "Steve, you have a tremendous outlook. How did you develop such a healthy attitude?"

"Well, I believe that in our lives we are all given glimpses of greatness, glimpses of the ability to really step beyond, to go one step outside our comfort zone. It is not only important to do it for ourselves, but it's important for us to do that for other people too. We need to be an inspiration for each other."

Steve is thirty-four years old. He has lived triumphantly with his disease for twenty years. He believes that God has healed him!

Oh God!
When I lost my love—
What a hole was left!
And the hole is so deep,
so empty, so dark, so black.

But the sun is going to rise again!
Until, at high noon it shall fill the
dark, empty hole with light,
warmth—love!

I'm waiting for the sunrise.
It's coming.
Nothing can stop it!

Hallelujah!
Amen.

Many of the people I've just told you about, who have
learned to find love and happiness in spite of enormous
obstacles, appear to be extraordinary. But in reality they are just
like you and me. They are people who have had pain and who
have hurt but have learned to rise above them.

How did they do it? Well, if you knew them as I know them,
you would see that they all have three things in common: 1) a
healthy love for themselves, 2) a harmonious love for God, and
3) a wholesome love for others.

As Jesus once said, "Love the LORD your God with all your
heart, with all your soul, and with all your mind . . . . [and]
your *neighbor as yourself*" (Matt. 22:37, 39, emphasis added).

Sound simple? It is. No matter what your situation, no
matter what your position, you can learn to love and be *loved*
that way. You can be loved! You can be happy—anyway!

JUNCTION ONE:

LOVE YOURSELF—
AND BE HAPPY!

"The happiest place on earth," they call it—Disneyland, California. I arrived in California in 1955, shortly before this joyous place opened only a mile and a half down the road from where later we built the Crystal Cathedral. The first thing Walt Disney built was the great communications loop, a railroad that encircled the park. Disneyland is many "lands"—Fantasyland, Frontierland, Adventureland, Tomorrowland—all tied together by the railroad. There are only a few stations. You can get on the train at any stop, but you will not experience fully the happiness of Disneyland if you get off the train at the first station you come to. It is very easy to be distracted by the alluring and enticing attractions and to disembark. You may revel in the fun at one station and forget that the clock is ticking. But later you will find out that your time has run out and you must leave the happy place and cannot finish the entire circle. Back at home you'd probably report, "Yes, I had great fun, but *no*, I didn't get a chance to have the full experience."

In much the same way, a life of happiness is found on the train called "love." There are three junctions. You can conceivably enter and exit at any of these three stations. One junction is called "Love Yourself and Be Happy!" Another is named "Love Your Neighbor and Be Happy!" A third carries the banner "Love God and Be Happy!"

In all cases love requires both giving and accepting: Love

flows when you *give* love to yourself, your neighbor, and your God and *accept* love from yourself, your neighbor, and your God.

You can enter the love train at any junction. But if you get sidetracked by the attractions and satisfactions and feel happy at any one stop and miss taking the whole trip, I must caution, even warn, you that the joy will only last if you make the entire loop.

But where does one really get on? Is it best to board at "Love God and Be Happy"? Perhaps. I know persons who have had amazing religious conversions. Before they learned to accept and love themselves or their neighbors, they were transformed by the love of God! This was their first experience with a nonjudgmental, nonmanipulative, honest, caring LOVE! For them this was the entry point to the happy life.

I know others who entered from the platform at "Love Your Neighbor and Be Happy!" They were confirmed agnostics or atheists, incapable of religious beliefs or feelings until they encountered authentic, unconditional love from another person. Malcom Muggeridge, the famed British author and television personality, comes to mind. While sipping tea in his cottage in Sussex, England, he once recounted to me how he was swept away by the love he saw in the life of Mother Teresa, a woman who personifies sacrificial love. Her love annihilated his cynicism, intellectual skepticism, and arrogant elitism and led him ultimately to a childlike faith in God.

"Love Yourself and Be Happy!" is the station where others step on the train. The primary hangup that kept these passengers from believing in love was their own lack of self-esteem or self-love. They were incapable of approaching God or others until they felt they had some value. So deep and entrenched was their lack of trust in their own potential value that they subconsciously turned off all loving signals sent their way. The first step these people needed to take, before they could have a happy experience in love, was to learn to love themselves.

WHERE SHOULD I GET ON?

There is a main entrance to the Disneyland railroad; it is at the front of the park, and if you had your choice of junctions, this would undoubtedly be the best place to get on the train. When it comes to the train of love, however, one can speculate, argue, study, which station on the love railroad, if any, is the central depot!

My specialty for thirty years has been a ministry passionately appealing to negative-thinking, impossibility thinkers who suffer from low self-esteem, lack of trust, and a profound lack of faith in themselves, in others, in God!

For that reason—call it strategy if you will—let's enter the "happy railroad that makes the love loop" at the station called "Love Yourself and Be Happy."

LOVE YOURSELF AND BE HAPPY

This station may not be the main entrance or the central depot or the most popular junction, but for many of us it is the place to begin. Until we can love ourselves, we'll never be able to love God or those around us.

———————— ❦ ❦ ————————

The Person Who Does Not Love Himself Is Too Empty Of Love To Give It Away . . . And Feels Too Unworthy To Accept It From God Or From Others.

———————— ❦ ❦ ————————

So I ask you now: "Do you love yourself?"

If your answer is a doubtful "yes" or a definite "no," then how can you expect others to love you? And if you don't believe others will love you, won't you miss the first sensitive signals of affection when they are sent your way? Won't you inadvertently nip love in the bud, in the first, fragile, tender stage?

Self-esteem is foundational. Therefore an inferiority complex is the first problem that has to be corrected! Before you can love or be loved—before you can ever hope to be happy—you need to achieve deep inner security. *You* have to discover your real intrinsic worth as a human being.

Self-love is an essential requirement for healthy living. It is a vital ingredient to long-lasting relationships. It is the key that can unlock the door to a life of genuine joy. Self-esteem is the deepest desire of our hearts.

Are you leery of this station because you wonder: *Will self-love lead to narcissism?* Narcissus, as you may know, was the Greek mythological character who tried to meet his need for self-esteem and self-love by *focusing on the material image of the self,* that is, the body. The material image of a person is what Swiss psychiatrist Paul Tournier calls the "personage." Narcissism focuses on the material solution to what is essentially a *spiritual* problem!

A great deal of "self-esteem" literature today misses the point right here! If loving yourself means admiring your body, your shape, your style of hair, your jewelry, clothing, or accessories, then indeed we are, like Narcissus, getting on the wrong track. Futility and frustration and eventual failure are the dismal, disillusioning, and despairing end to the counterfeit self-esteem offered by narcissism. At best it is cosmetic psychology, and what is needed is not a cosmetic treatment, but conversion: The heart of a human must be changed!

I must believe that I have value as a person! No matter who I am, I can be an encourager! I can be a spreader of hope! I can be a spirit-lifter to disheartened people! I can be a conduit, a channel for God's love, joy, and peace to flow to other human beings! I can love others and myself with God's love! I *can* do it, if I'll be a *conduit!*

The truth is that any person who has achieved self-love based on sacrificial love for others has acquired the best preventive treatment against narcissism.

A favorite picture of mine in my study is a picture of only the folded hands of Mother Teresa. I love it. The fingernails are all broken! Unfiled! Here then is a portrait of spiritual, healthy, self-love. Can you see any narcissism in it?

You may be cautious at the "Love Yourself—and Be Happy" station because *you were taught that self-love will lead to pride.* Wait a minute! If that thought holds you back from loving yourself, you are a victim of the frailties of language.

What we need to realize is that *pride* is a word in the English language that is both positive and negative. Therefore, it is confusing and dangerous. Destructive, *negative* pride is the very opposite of self-love. It is arrogance! It is egotism—the very opposite of self-esteem.

But *positive* pride generates tremendous generosity! A strong self-respect motivates a person to unselfish liberality! Only persons with an abundance of inner spiritual resources dare to give themselves away, investing their love and caring in a variety of human lives. Only these persons can afford to lose!

Perhaps, you are afraid of this station because *you have been mistreated, maligned, rejected, and hurt by people you loved.* A young woman named Mary I once knew would understand how you feel. A bride-to-be, Mary had mailed the invitations to her wedding weeks earlier. Her dress and the gowns of her four attendants were already purchased. The wedding cake, baked and frosted, was waiting to be cut the following day. She was wrapping her gift for the groom when the telephone rang. It was he! "Mary." The voice was strained.

"Hi, John. Aren't you excited?" she asked.

"Mary," he continued painfully, "I can't go through with it. I mean it's all off. There isn't going to be a wedding tomorrow. Don't ask questions. I'm sorry. Goodbye."

The stunned young woman went to her pastor's office.

"What is wrong with me? I know there must be something terribly wrong," she said. Her slender shoulders trembled as her head dropped. "I'm so embarrassed. I can't face anyone anymore. Somewhere, I failed terribly."

I have heard virtually the same words from a man who had just come through a divorce; from the mother of three children whose husband had quietly deserted her; from a millionaire who had suffered financial reverses and subsequent bankruptcy; from an executive who was mysteriously "let go" from a firm he had served faithfully for years; and from more alcoholics than I can remember.

When these kinds of life situations hit and you feel inept and unsure of yourself, you can recapture lost confidence. A way out and up is always possible.

Go for it! Get on the train. Head for the junction, "Love Yourself and Be Happy." Discover in the process the rebirth of your self-worth.

A REBIRTH OF SELF-WORTH

No matter what has happened in your life you are *not* a "complete failure," a "hopeless sinner," a "total washout." After twenty years in the field of people-counseling I have heard that exaggerated, distorted, destructive lie repeated many hundreds of times, and a lie quickly becomes a truth if you believe it. In almost every instance I was able to see and point out worthwhile qualities in the person who was unfairly, unreasonably, and unlovingly self-condemning.

There are vast undamaged areas in every human life. You will discover them in this station if you will board the train one step at a time.

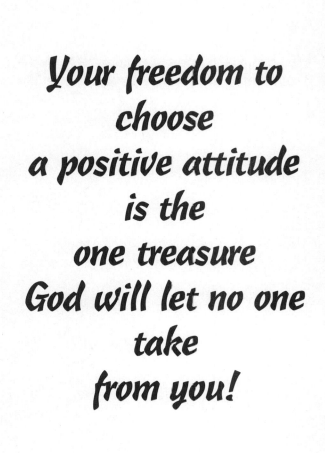

Your freedom to
choose
a positive attitude
is the
one treasure
God will let no one
take
from you!

Step I. Stop Putting Yourself Down!

It is important to realize that although you may not be able to change what has happened, you *can* control how you *react* to what has happened. Remember that you will never again be the person you were before you experienced any trauma. You have two options. You can decide that you have nothing left to live for. Or you can say, "I may have failed, but I am still a person of worth."

Self-debasing thoughts will come naturally to your mind. Restrain them. Whatever you do, do not believe them. They are extreme, emotional exaggerations. By all means, resist the destructive inclination to welcome, nurse, feed, and strengthen these self-destroying feelings. The depressed person tends to strengthen self-debasing thinking by deliberately choosing to believe the worst about himself. The emotionally "down" individual deliberately goes on a self-degrading mental rampage—listing all the failures ever encountered; pointing up all the weaknesses; recalling from the long-forgotten past any and every blunder ever made.

In this crazy, self-destroying mental activity, the depressed man or woman—

- Exaggerates the significance and the reality of these real or fancied shortcomings.
- Accepts personal blame almost entirely and mercilessly for all these failures, stubbornly refusing to believe or remember how other persons contributed to the mistakes.
- Makes certain worthy virtues and accomplishments are forgotten or discredited and belittles, berates, and betrays noble character qualities. The value or the reality of all the positive qualities in this person's life is angrily scorned when some friend calls attention to them.

Why do we tend to despair and further degrade ourselves with self-destructive thinking? Are we seeking sympathy to nurse our wounded pride? Do we hate ourselves so much that we want to mentally liquidate, eliminate, and eradicate that which we hate? Does an irrational subconscious suppose that it will love itself if it mentally destroys the self it hates? Or are we trying to atone for the guilt of failure? Do we deliberately inflict this mental punishment upon ourselves, hoping finally to awaken a feeling that we are redeemed through the crucifixion of self-condemnation? Whatever the reason, it is important to understand that we cannot rebuild self-love by destroying the undamaged areas of self-worth that still remain.

Step II. Select Self-respect, Not Self-pity!

You certainly do not rebuild self-love by indulging in self-pity. Self-pity focuses on the unhappy past, keeping alive the very experiences which must be forgotten and left behind. Self-pity focuses on what has happened. While you are concentrating on the unfortunate past, you are in that moment enslaved, controlled, and dominated by the self-demoralizing past. Something regrettable may have happened, but don't allow yourself to *remain* trapped in that experience by self-pity.

If unpleasant things come to pass, by all means let them pass! Quit holding on.

Why are we so inclined to self-pity? Are we trying to tenderly nurse a wounded ego? If so, we must see that self-pity only keeps the wounded pride raw and open. In our own self-pity we hope to gain the pity of others, mistaking sympathy for respect. We crave to reassure the faltering self that it is worthy after all.

Or do we indulge in self-pity—trapping ourselves in the past—for fear of moving ahead into the future where we might suffer additional assaults? Is self-pity a deceptive defense mechanism willfully experienced to protect us from new risks we may encounter if we start to think of beginning again?

You will never rebuild self-love until you *liberate yourself from self-pity and the tyranny of unpleasant memories.* You must stop thinking and talking about them. *Do not allow them to control you.* Banish such thoughts as "I'm finished . . . I'm a failure . . . I'll never do anything worthwhile . . . I bungled every chance I had . . . I hate myself . . . I'll never amount to anything."

When such thoughts occur, REMEMBER:

Failure Is No Disgrace

It takes courage to try. It is more honorable to try something worthwhile and fail than never to attempt any worthy venture. Play-it-safe people seldom win the applause and the respect of others; they never do anything to merit congratulations!

I have a motto that applies to this:

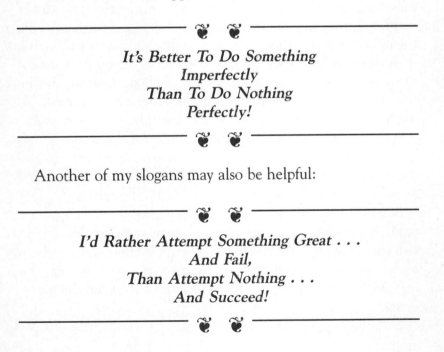

It's Better To Do Something
Imperfectly
Than To Do Nothing
Perfectly!

Another of my slogans may also be helpful:

I'd Rather Attempt Something Great . . .
And Fail,
Than Attempt Nothing . . .
And Succeed!

If you have tried but don't feel you have succeeded, you should feel proud of yourself! You are great! You had the courage to dream! You had the guts to try! You have succeeded in dreaming!

Failure Is Proof That I'm a Human Being

Tell yourself—"If I have suffered failure, I am in good company. I can be sure that I am a member of the human race!"

Every person has failed somewhere, even if it was the failure to see and seize a great opportunity. That often is the most costly, although unrevealed, failure.

Nobody's perfect. Yet everybody seems to have an inclination to be perfect. They wish they were perfect or they would like to give people the impression that they're perfect.

The truth is: *Everybody's imperfect*, but most people don't want to admit it. And average human beings go through a lot of mental and social games, wearing masks, trying to give people the impression that they are almost faultless. The tragedy is that such persons never become authentic. The most beautiful thing to me about the gospel is that it shows how we can be accepted by God even though we are imperfect and sinful.

One of the exciting things about the Bible is that it makes perfectly clear that the great people whom God used were far from perfect. For instance, Noah was a drunkard. Moses committed murder. Joseph was arrogant. David, who was called a "man after God's own heart," was guilty of adultery.

Now, if these great men of God conspicuously, glaringly, and publicly had their sins and imperfections, yet God was able to redeem, change, and use them, I suggest this ought to be a source of great encouragement to you and me! We can be reassured that *nobody is perfect*. Everybody sins, even the nicest people.

In love's service—only broken hearts qualify . . .

P.S. Have you earned your credentials?

Failure Can Be Fruitful

If my failures teach me something, they will have positive value. I can learn from my weaknesses. I can learn something about other people or, if nothing more, I can learn patience, compassion, and humility. A failure may turn out to be the greatest thing that ever happened to me.

Have you had a failure? Has your company gone under? Has your marriage fallen apart? Have you been stood up at the altar? Have you lost a loved one through death? Is your heart breaking?

Is there someone who needs you, who could benefit from what you learned through your pain? Your loss? Your failure?

"Turn Your Scars into Stars," by turning your hurts into halos, by using your pain to help ease somebody else's.

When my daughter Sheila was in her freshman year at Hope College in Holland, Michigan, three thousand miles away from home, she went through a devastating experience.

Because of an overflow attendance at the college that year, nine freshmen, along with a dorm resident advisor, were housed in a cottage (an old home adjacent to the campus). These nine freshmen didn't know a soul when they stepped on that campus. And thrown together as they were, they formed a tightly knit group.

Their personalities were as different as night from day, and their interests and values were also frequently dissimilar, but since they lived separately from the other students the friendships grew.

One of the girls, Linda, was not the easiest person to get along with. She was outspoken and sometimes surly. She seemed to be groping for identity and affection and always had a tough shell around her, though there were times when she seemed to be daring someone to crack it. One night she approached my daughter and said, "Sheila, do you really believe in God? I mean, you're always reading your Bible and stuff, and I know your father's a minister, but do you *really* believe in God? Do you feel Him deep down inside?"

Sheila looked at Linda with surprise. Linda had made no pretenses about where she stood on such matters as religion, dating, and drugs.

"Yes, Linda," Sheila answered, "I do believe in God. And I do feel Him deep down inside. I know He loves me as much as I love Him. Do you believe in God, Linda?"

Linda burst out, "I wish I could! I really wish I could!" And off she ran to her room. Although Sheila tried to talk to her further, Linda made it clear that the discussion was over.

One afternoon when Sheila arrived home from studying she was greeted by one of the other girls who said, "Oh, Sheila! It's terrible! It's so terrible!"

"What is it? What's happened?" Sheila asked.

"It's Linda! We don't know if she's going to make it or not!"

"What do you mean?"

"She took a whole lot of pills. She's in the hospital. She's in a coma."

Sheila was stunned. She prayed, "Oh Linda! You've got to make it! There's still so much I have to tell you about Jesus and His love for you!"

Providentially, I was at the college at that time for a board meeting. Sheila ran along the icy sidewalks across the campus to the hall where the board was meeting. Sheila stood outside the room and prayed frantically for the meeting to end. Finally, when a student aide brought me a message that Sheila wanted to see me, I hurried out of the meeting to find my daughter looking visibly shaken. She buried herself in my arms and poured out the whole tragic story.

I took her by the arm and led her out to a lone sidewalk where we could walk off the grief and talk without interruption.

Finally, I said, "Sheila, trouble never leaves you where it finds you. It will either leave you a bitter person or a better person. Do you remember the phrase I taught you, 'In love's service, only broken hearts will do'?"

"Yes."

"Well, you are experiencing today the real hurt and agony that comes with a broken heart. Only people who have experienced what you are feeling now can be compassionate enough to help others. Let God take your hurt and use it to make you a better person, a special person—one who's fit for love's service."

As Sheila told me later, "I resolved then and there not to let Linda's life go to waste. No matter what the outcome, whether she lived or died, I would let God use the hurt."

Linda's life hung in the balance for three days. One night, the chaplain came over and met with the girls in the living room of their cottage. "She's gone," he said.

Linda's life was short, but it had a tremendous impact on Sheila's. In fact for seven years after she graduated from college Sheila worked as a counselor to troubled young girls in our church. She spent her summers working with girls at campgrounds and took numerous young girls under her wing, becoming a big sister to many.

Sheila told me, "In my life I have seen many 'Lindas.' Most of them have not physically taken their lives, but many of them are dying inside. Whenever I see a girl who is hurting, confused, or lost, I remember Linda; and I remember your words, Dad: 'In love's service, only broken hearts will do.' And then I know what to do. I can sign up for love's service, for I know how fatal a broken heart can be."

Just because it looks as if you have failed, it doesn't necessarily mean that you still won't succeed. So don't give up! Don't make an irreversible negative decision that you may later regret.

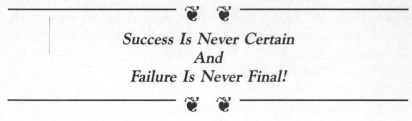

*Success Is Never Certain
And
Failure Is Never Final!*

Remember those words. Burn them into your subconscious. A time will come when you will need them.

Several years ago, when the "Hour of Power" first went on television, we gave away a most challenging gift. Knowing that the olive trees in California were originally from the Holy Land, we knew a tiny olive tree would be special and precious to our viewers. The gift was attractive, helpful, and within our budget, but it was next to impossible to package and mail!

After making the offer we were overwhelmed with tens of thousands of requests for the tiny olive trees. The trees were sent. Two weeks later we were deluged with tons of negative mail. To our dismay most of the trees had arrived dead or dried out. But one letter impressed me:

My Dear Friend,

I have received the olive tree and wish to thank you. Permit me to take a moment of your precious time to tell you about my experience. What a thrill I had when the postman delivered the little box. I was so excited and happy. I gently opened the carton and to my surprise found a plastic bag with a tiny plastic box and a dried-out twig! What a letdown! I could have cried. I felt as though this little innocent olive tree had smothered and withered inside this plastic bag on the long trip from California to New York.

Well, I read the instructions carefully and for some reason I didn't throw it away. I transplanted that olive twig. While doing this I felt so sorry for it because it had dried out and withered and the leaves were folded down. Most had fallen off. I soaked the poor twig thoroughly and placed it on a table facing the east sun. I felt foolish keeping this twig and giving it so much attention. But after several days, a surprise! The leaves had lifted and a tiny branch had turned itself to the sun.

I am so delighted now, words can't express my gratitude to you. I just love it.

I wonder how many olive trees were thrown away as dead twigs because people didn't have the faith to believe there was still life in those withered roots?

Is your life bare? Has a dream died? Has your self-esteem been shattered? Don't throw it all away! Don't give up yet! There's still life in the roots. Tap into them. Drench them with faith in yourself and in God.

Failure Is Never Total

"I'm a *complete* failure," the self-degrading person wrongly claims. But *no* person is ever a *total* failure!

Any person who claims complete worthlessness is absolutely wrong. The late Dr. Smiley Blanton, an eminent psychiatrist, once said to his colleague Norman Vincent Peale; "There are vast undamaged areas in every human life. These undamaged areas must be discovered, then used as the base for a new beginning."

Psychiatrists have long noted that mental illness never seems to be total. Freud wrote that even patients with severe hallucinations later reported that "in some corner of their minds," as they expressed it, "there was a normal person hidden, who watched the progress of the illness go past like a detached spectator."

In World War II an asylum in France that housed 158 persons considered hopelessly and incurably insane was liberated by advancing armies. All the inmates escaped. Years later it was discovered that fifty-three were living normal lives, apparently recovered.

No matter what your condition—you *can* rebuild a meaningful future! You *can* reconstruct a self-love-generating life.

Step III. Start Believing in Yourself!

You only have one more step to climb before your self worth will be reborn! It is time to act! You must believe in *you!*

You are filled with many wonderful possibilities. Look for them! You will be amazed at what you will discover.

Discover Your True Identity

Look at the history of the great families: the Medicis of Italy, the Hapsburgs of Germany, and the Stuarts of England. You may say, "If I carried one of those family names and had that identification and those connections, I'd really be somebody. I know I would have self-esteem."

Well, I have good news for you. You can be identified with the family of God. God can be your father! If God's your father, and you're His child, you must be somebody terrific! You carry His honorable name!

During the French Revolution on separate occasions King Louis XVI and Queen Marie Antoinette were escorted to the guillotine in a square in Paris and beheaded. A tale is told that at one of the executions the crowd watching went crazy, screaming joyously! "Bring out the prince!" they bellowed. "He's next!" The young boy was terrified! He was only eight years old, but he was to be the next king and so the mob thought he had to be eliminated, too. He stood on the platform trembling in his black velvet coat and patent leather shoes. His golden curls, which fell over his shoulders, were damp from his tears. "Down with him! Kill all kings!" screamed the furious horde.

But then out of the crowd came a vicious voice. "Don't kill him! You'll only send his soul to heaven. That's too good for royalty. I say, turn him over to Meg, the old witch! She'll teach him filthy words. She'll teach him to be a sinner. And then, when he dies his soul will go to hell! That's what royalty deserves!"

So, according to legend, that's exactly what happened. The officials turned the young prince over to Meg, the witch. But every time she tried to teach him vulgarities, the prince stubbornly stamped his little feet until his curls shook, and with clenched fists he said, "I will not say it! I will not say those dirty words! I was born to be a King, and I won't talk that way!"

The problem with many people today is that they don't realize who they are. If you are a child of God, *He's your father!* Do you feel close enough to God to call Him your father? Do you feel close enough to go to Him at any time for any reason? I have five children by birth. They can come to me anytime. They have inside connections. They have my most private, unlisted telephone number. I am their father! They are my children. *You* can have that kind of relationship with God!

Discover Your Innate Dignity

When you know who you are, you will live an ennobled life! When you have a tremendous sense of self-respect, you won't stoop to crime; you won't use profane language; you won't abuse the people around you. It will be beneath your dignity. There are some things that the Schuller family doesn't do. It's the same way with God's family. When you consciously know that you belong to the family of God, you develop the most healing, helpful, and divine sense of righteous pride. It will not be a sinful pride; it will be a redemptive pride.

Let me illustrate this with a story I read in high school years ago. A farmer's young son had been outside playing one day and came home with a large, odd-looking egg. The boy proudly showed it to his father and asked if he could keep it. The farmer didn't know exactly what to do with it, so he went to the barn and carefully placed it under a mother goose that was nesting. A few days later the father and son were leaving the house when they saw the mother goose parading across the barnyard followed by six beautiful baby geese. It was a comical sight, because the tiny newborn creatures were trying frantically to keep up with their mother.

The boy and his father smiled and started to turn around . . . but then something caught their eyes. One little goose was trailing behind the rest. His beak was not flat, it was pointed and twisted. He could hardly walk, because he had claws instead of delicate webbed feet. Instead of having lovely white plumes, he was an ugly brown color. And to top it off, he made a terrible squawking sound. He was a freaky bird, ugly and disfigured!

Then one day, above the barnyard flew a giant eagle. He swept lower and lower until the strange, awkward little bird on the ground lifted his head and pointed his crooked beak into the sky to see what it was. The misfit creature then stretched his wings and began to hobble across the yard. He flapped his wings harder and harder until the wind picked him up and carried him higher and higher. He began to soar through the clouds! He discovered what he was! He had been born to be an eagle, but he was trying to live like a goose!

You were born to soar! You were created in God's image! The tragedy is that too many human beings have never discovered their divine heritage so they live like animals. God loves you— He created you—you are His child. Do you know it? Have you claimed your divine heritage?

Discover Your Latent Possibilities

Every situation contains within it the seed of a possibility. If you were born in poverty, if you are part of a minority, if you apparently lack resources—don't give up on yourself. You have possibilities within and around you. Look for them. Discover them. It may be to show compassion; it may be to help somebody who is hurting. In the process you will be blessed because problems combined with possibility thinking can propel you to do great things. And when you have overcome obstacles and turned problems into opportunities, you will be amazed at how good you will begin to feel about yourself.

Discover Your Unique Ability

Everybody has been created with a special gift, a very personal, unique ability to do something great for God. And until you discover exactly what it is that makes you special, you will feel inadequate, insecure, even inferior. It's up to you to discover what it is that makes you the wonderful person you are. It's up to you to take inventory of your talents, gifts, and unique abilities.

One word of caution. Many people get hung up on the word *talent*—they think it's something you are born with. I contend that frequently talent is something you acquire, like experience or wisdom. It can be developed through hard work, like studying. Frequently, talent is spelled W-O-R-K.

Sherrill Milnes is the leading baritone of the Metropolitan Opera, as well as of the other leading opera houses of the world, and a good friend who has sung magnificently for us in the Crystal Cathedral. This famous singer was the son of a preacher, born and reared, like me, on a farm in the Midwest.

Anybody who has been reared on a farm knows all about the work ethic. It is drilled into a child from early in life as the entire family works together from sunup to sundown, milking the cows, feeding the various animals, gathering eggs, pitching hay, working the fields. I asked Sherrill once when we were together, "Do you think your boyhood farm experience affected you any way in your successful career?"

Sherrill smiled and said in his deep baritone voice, "I think it did very definitely. Life on a small family farm teaches you the value of hard work, and personally I think that the only way that one can fulfill his talent and his ambitions is to work at it."

"But, Sherrill," I said, "I think most people look at you and say, 'Well, you've got the talent. You just open your mouth and sing.'"

"Oh, that's just not true!" he replied. "It takes a lot of work and a great deal of discipline to be a leading singer with the Metropolitan Opera Company. I vocalize *daily*. I also have to take good care of my instrument, my voice, which is with me wherever I go, of course. That means I have to make sure that I get plenty of rest. If performances are scheduled too close together, I have to be careful that I budget enough time for that rest and for rehearsals. *Talent*, you see, is *hard work, discipline, common sense*, and *keeping yourself in good physical and mental shape*."

Recently I had dinner with famed lawyer Louis Nizer. He said to me, "I have often lectured at the greatest law schools in America. At those lectures I enjoy telling the students—'I want to introduce you to a mystic word. It will perform miracles for you. It will open portals for you. This marvelous, mystic word will turn the *stupid* student into a *bright* student, the *bright* student into a *brilliant* student, the *brilliant* student into a *steadfast* student! This word will guarantee great success for anyone. The mystic word is W-O-R-K!'"

Talent? *Everybody* has it! Hard work? *Anybody* can apply themselves diligently if they decide they really want to. Discipline? It's just a choice between doing what will make you feel better about yourself or doing what will make you angry with yourself.

You can be somebody special! In fact, you *are* somebody special! It's up to you to find out what it is you're especially good at, and then do it the very best you can. It may be to sing like Sherrill Milnes. It may be to listen. After all, what good is a singer without an audience?

Your talent is not more nor less important than the talent of someone else. God made you—*YOU*—for a special reason. Ask Him to show you what that is.

Discover Your Divine Destiny

"For I know the plans I have for you, says the Lord. They are plans for good and not for evil, to give you a future and a hope."

(Jer. 29:11 TLB)

This Bible verse says plainly that God has a plan and a dream and it includes you. You were born for a purpose. You are here for a reason. When you discover God's dream for your life, then you will be well on your way to discovering your worth as a fellow human being, sharing this planet called earth.

Donna Stone Pesche discovered her destiny, and millions of children will now live without fear and pain because of her efforts. You may have heard of Donna. Her father, W. Clement Stone, is renowned for his many contributions to worthy projects, as well as his P.M.A. (Positive Mental Attitude) seminars and books.

Donna died from cancer in 1985, but not before she was able

to set in motion the National Committee for Prevention of Child Abuse. Donna was always interested in child welfare and children with unmet needs, but her greatest motivation came from the fact that her mother, Jesse, had been an abused child. Jesse's last remembrance of her father was the police taking him away after he had chased her mother with a butcher knife. When Donna heard that story, it made such an impression on her that she decided to do whatever she could to prevent all kinds of abuse, but especially child abuse.

As Donna said to me in 1981, "Reverend Schuller, child abuse is a tremendous problem. We believe that child abuse affects over a million children every year in the United States. And we estimate that it kills at least five thousand to seven thousand children a year. It's a tremendous problem. Next to sudden infant death and accidents, abuse is the number one killer of children in America."

"What kinds of people would beat a child?" I asked Donna.

"These parents are not monsters. They are people who have their own unmet needs. I like to think of them as people who have only half a cup. If you have almost nothing emotionally, it's so hard to give to other people. They are usually people who are immature, who have a very low sense of self-esteem. They have no pride in themselves. Usually, they have been abused as children themselves. They are people who have unrealistic expectations of their own children. And they are people who are suffering, in crisis, and need help."

"What can be done to help prevent child abuse?" I asked.

"Well," Donna said, "as more people become aware of the problem, we hope and pray that the problem will gradually diminish. Certainly, it must get better, for we have found that 90 percent of the people incarcerated in the prison system have been victims of abuse or gross neglect. So we have to work with children. Another way we're trying to help is by starting self-help groups, like Parents Anonymous. Your help-line, 'NEW HOPE,' [at the Crystal Cathedral] is an excellent prevention."

Perfect love
perceives
people—
not as problems!
But—
as possibilities!

Only a few years after this conversation took place, Donna discovered she had breast cancer—shortly after my wife, Arvella, lost a breast to cancer. I remember Arvella's calling Donna and praying with her, supporting her in the tough struggle against this horrible disease.

Then I remember my last meeting with Donna. I was told she could meet me at the Admiral's Club of American Airlines at O'Hare Airport. By now she was battling the cancer furiously, and because the treatments had caused a hair loss, she wore a turban over her head. She was as vivacious as ever! We went to her home. She told me the cancer had entered her brain. I looked at her and said, "Oh, Donna, you can still see."

"Yes!"

"You can still hear."

"Yes!"

"You can still talk."

"Yes!"

"You can still feel." She had her hands on mine and I had mine on hers.

"Yes!"

She interrupted me and said, "But, Dr. Schuller, best of all, I can still *give!*"

This was the secret to Donna's sense of self-worth. She had discovered her destiny. She had discovered what she was meant to give to the world. And she derived a tremendous amount of joy and self-esteem from giving of herself to others until the very end of her life.

NOW—BELIEVE IN YOURSELF AND BE HAPPY

- YOU have your own *identity;* none of us is exactly alike.
- YOU have your own unique fingerprints; YOU can make your own unique impression on the world!

- YOU have an innate sense of *dignity*. Do not suppress it. Cultivate it! Hold your head up high.
- YOU have latent *possibilities*. Find a need and fill it. With all the hurt in the world today, there is no excuse for feeling useless.
- YOU have unique *ability*. YOU can find it if YOU will look in the right places.
- YOU have a divine *destiny*. YOU were created with a specific purpose in mind. God chose someone special—YOU! He believes in someone special—YOU!

God believes in YOU. YOU can, too.

So take the first step: Head for the love train. Enter at the station "Love Yourself and Be Happy!"

JUNCTION TWO:
LOVE GOD— AND BE HAPPY!

"I would love to believe in God, if I knew it was the truth," an intelligent young Japanese said to me as I finished a lecture in Tokyo. He continued, "*Prove* God to me. That's what the unbelieving world is waiting for. We're scientific. We want *proof* before we believe."

"But that's a contradiction," I answered. "If there is proof, there is no longer room for belief. For faith believes in that which cannot be proven." I looked into this bright young man's shining black eyes and said, "Let me put it this way:

WHEN PROOF IS POSSIBLE, FAITH
BECOMES IMPOSSIBLE!
AND WHEN PROOF IS IMPOSSIBLE, FAITH
BECOMES POSSIBLE!"

At this second junction of the Happy Railroad we will see that loving God is a two-fold process. We need to *believe* in God and we need to *love* Him. We need to deal with our *beliefs* as well as our *feelings* about our Creator. We do that when we make a commitment of our whole being—mind, will, and emotions to God. And so we will obtain our ticket at this station when we choose to believe, and we will board the train when we begin to love our Creator.

PICK UP YOUR TICKET—CHOOSE
TO BELIEVE!

Now let me say this—*if you are looking for proof about God*—you will not be able to board the Love Train at this station—and if you boarded the railroad at some other stop, your journey on this loop of love will be stopped by derailment at this point. You need to choose to believe if you want to explore and discover true love and genuine joy. You do have three options open to you, you know:

1. There is *a* God. This is theism.
2. There is *no* God. This is atheism.
3. "I don't know; therefore I'm not going to commit either way." This is agnosticism.

It's important to be honest when discussing the existence of God, for there is no firm, final proof for any position. Both theist and atheist have made commitments to a belief system without conclusive proof.

The atheists and the theists both are believers and have faith. The difference is: Atheists are negative in their faith; theists are positive in their faith. The atheist says "No." The theist says "Yes." The atheist says "There is nothing." The theist says "There is something."

The atheist says "All believers in God, without a single exception, in all of human history have been mistaken. I am wiser than they. I say they were wrong, I am right!"

The theist says "All believers in God, in all of human history, cannot *all* without a single exception have been wrong! What if they are right? I could make a tragic error if I arrogantly reject their collective testimony! Jesus Christ believed in God! I suspect He knew something we don't! I'll trust Jesus in humble faith before I'll trust the atheist."

The honest fact is either there is a God or there is not a God.

Either the theist or the atheist is right. Both at least have the courage to take a stand. This is more than can be said for the agnostic. He runs with the hares and dashes with the hounds. He vacillates and remains indecisive. Proudly he applauds himself for "rising above the battle." In fact he cowardly avoids an issue that will not go away. *No* decision is certainly not the *right* decision. The evasive position of the agnostic is surely not an answer. And does any bright, sensitive person want to go through an entire lifetime avoiding or evading life's ultimate question for fear of making the wrong decision?

This choice to believe will require honesty and courage. To be honest is to admit that there are no final proofs. To be courageous is to choose to believe—anyway!

For those of you who are afraid of appearing ignorant if you believe in God, let me remind you that many of the world's greatest scientists are believers in God. Take Dr. Michael DeBakey, for example, who is one of the world's leading heart surgeons. His accomplishments in the last forty-nine years have led to revolutionary advances in treatment for cardiovascular diseases. Dr. DeBakey created the pump that makes open-heart surgery possible and has developed more than fifty different surgical instruments. You can't go into a surgical room anywhere in the world without picking up an instrument that bears the name "DeBakey."

What drives this man? What motivates him? If you ask him, he'll tell you it's his faith in God and his faith in humanity. I recently had the privilege of meeting this great man. I took hold of his hands and asked him, "Dr. DeBakey, how many human hearts have these hands held?"

He said, "Oh, over fifty thousand."

I thought, *fifty thousand? That can't be! He'd have to perform over eleven hundred surgeries a year. That's got to be impossible!*

Just then he said, "Dr. Schuller, I have a surgery going on right now. I think you'd like to see it. It's in Dome 4."

I followed him through a door that opened onto a balcony. I looked down through a glass ceiling into an operating room. Suddenly I understood how he had done it! Surgeries were going on in Domes 1, 2, 3, and 4. He moved from one team of surgeons in one room, to the next, to the next, and to the next. Fifty thousand hearts was probably an understatement!

For the first time, from my perch on the balcony, I looked down at a man who was having open-heart surgery. All I could see was a table, surrounded by nine doctors and three nurses, all wearing green masks. The table was covered with green cloth. There in the middle of all this green was something that resembled a bowl. In that bowl was a huge red chunk of something that was moving. I said, "Dr. DeBakey, could that be a living human heart?"

"Yes!"

"His *living* heart?"

"I hope so," he said with a chuckle. Then Dr. DeBakey looked at me, put his arm around me, and said with a moist eye, "Bob, look at that! Isn't it beautiful? What a temple! I have done this for forty-nine years, and not once have I failed to feel the presence of God when I have seen the heart.

Faith in God! Some of the most intelligent men and women in the world have decided that the smartest choice to make is to believe in a God—of *love*—no less!

"I WANT TO BELIEVE—BUT I HAVE QUESTIONS!"

Our faith—although it is a leap over the chasms where proofs elude us—is not *blind*. It is based on solid evidence and premises. As a pastor I am aware of the three major questions that many people struggle with.

Question #1: If There Is a God—Why Did He Put Everything on a Faith-only Basis?

The answer to this question is simply that God wanted to allow us to be possibility thinkers, persons, believers—not puppets nor computers. The Bible says that the human being was designed to be a decision-making creature. That's the meaning of Adam and Eve. God deliberately gives us the choice to obey or disobey, because if there is no choice, there is no development of character. Unless there is more than one possibility offered, we will never learn to live by faith. Faith is choosing a possibility before we can be sure that it's the right one.

Living life on the faith-only basis is what makes life worth living. It gives life its meaning.

Faith is often called a "leap." How appropriate! How else could you possibly move from one point to another when there is no direct link? How else do you cross over a crevice when there is no bridge?

Faith is leaping across gaps that exist between:

- the known and the unknown;
- the proven and the unproven;
- the actual and the possible;
- the grasp and the reach;
- the "I've got it" and the "I want it";
- the knowledge and the mystery;
- sin and forgiveness;
- life and death;
- time and eternity.

Faith is making decisions before you've solved all of the problems.

Faith is making commitments before you can be assured everything will work out right.

Faith is moving ahead before you have answers to all the questions.

Faith is taking a risk without being fully insured.

Faith is choosing to believe before there is total proof.

You Will _Never_ Have _All_ the Answers!

If we are open-mindedly seeking the truth about life and God, we must leave room for mysteries and unanswered questions. Life and religion is a compilation of facts and mysteries. Even science has to leave room for mystery.

And thank God for mystery! If we knew _all_ the answers, if we knew the way everything worked, how boring, how cold, how calculating life would be. Perhaps you've heard the little ditty that shows this so succinctly:

> Twinkle, twinkle little star,
> I know exactly what you are:
> An incandescent ball of gas,
> Condensing to a solid mass!

The Negative Answers You Have May Be Wrong!

Louis Kahn, the great architect, once said, "If when I am ready to begin a new project, if I then have all the answers, some of my answers are wrong."

Check the neat little negative answers you have lived with so long. What if those answers are wrong and others' answers are right? Do you want to go to your grave having lived your entire life by the wrong answers? "O.K.," you say, "but how do I know if my answers are right or wrong?"

Well, if an answer is right, it will check out. If your bank book is accurate it will balance. If a scientific deduction is correct, it will fit the test results. If you doubt that God's love exists I challenge you to consider some evidence I have gathered.

In my work I have blessed thousands upon thousands of human beings with a look, a word, and a touch. Some have been in wheelchairs, some with crutches, some with limbs missing. Some speak with difficulty because of brain damage incurred in accidents. And yet, in spite of the pain, in spite of the difficulties, in spite of the battles with cancer and other physical infirmities, these people—who have every reason to be bitter, depressed, and angry at the world and at God—are *genuinely happy.* How do you explain that?

Sure, they still hurt. Yes, there is still pain. But beyond that there is HAPPINESS! Why? Because they all believe that they are truly loved. They believe that God loves them. And that authentic, real love gives them the reason for their joy. They have chosen to believe in this positive answer to the awesome, often troubling questions we all have about life.

If you cannot believe in a God of love, perhaps you are living with the wrong answers. There are people who do believe in happiness, in goodness, in *love!* What if these people are right? What if you are wrong?

Question #2: How Can I Believe in a God of Love in an Evil World?

That's the wrong question! The right question is, *"How can I doubt God in a world that is this good?"*

Now! I ask you, which question is the more constructive? Creative? Redemptive?

If we're going to find faith we need to get an accurate, positive perception of reality. It is true that:

- The world is filled with suffering!
- We are surrounded by selfish people!
- The world is under the threat of missiles, terrorism, and thermonuclear destruction.

However, it is *also* true that there is a lot of good in the world! There is suffering. There is selfishness. But there is also an immense capacity for love within the human family.

Ken Kragen is wonderful evidence of this. Ken was the driving force behind "We Are the World" and "USA for Africa." Ken, who is the manager for such star performers as Kenny Rogers and Lionel Richie, gathered together his clients and many other entertainers to record a song that raised nearly $50 million for the starving people in Africa.

As Ken shared with me the excitement of this incredible feat he said, "I went to Africa with the first shipment of food and supplies, and when I came back, everywhere I went in this great country people said to me, 'That's wonderful what we're doing for Africa. It's necessary—it is important—but we have things here at home that need to be done. When are we going to do something for America?' Then I knew we had to do something even bigger for our own country."

Ken did that with "Hands Across America." On May 25, 1986, millions of Americans stood hand to hand in a glorious link-up from the Pacific Ocean to the Atlantic Ocean. The chain wound its way through the Crystal Cathedral during our Sunday service. We joined hands in this incredible outpouring of love to make a difference in this country. All of the money raised was given to the homeless and hungry right here in America.

"What I have seen, Dr. Schuller, through all of this," Ken said, "is that *people want to give*. People do care enough to do something for those less fortunate."

I applaud Ken Kragen. "Hands Across America" represents

the best of American tradition, where we care about our neighbor—we help, we build a house, we rebuild the barn that burned down. During my childhood my family lost everything in a tornado; I remember what it was like when people brought us blankets, clothes, and food.

People like Ken Kragen are proof of the fact that "God loves you and so do I!" Look around you. Anytime you show me a horrific tragedy, I will show you an example of tremendous compassion. Always remember *to check the love that is in the human race*—love that is unquenchable! Indestructible!

There is a wonderful Bible verse (Song of Sol. 8:7) that I learned as a boy:

> Many waters cannot quench love
> Nor can the floods drown it.

"Waters" such as hurt, deceit, anger, and bitterness exist— they threaten to destroy love. But time and again, history has proven that love is the stronger force. Love always wins out in the end.

There is a love loose in this world that no amount of evil can ever imprison. And so long as there is love, I must believe in a God who will never let love die.

Question #3: How Can I Believe in a God of Love When Personal Tragedy Overwhelms Me, When "All Hell Breaks Loose"?

Again, I must ask: What's your perception of reality? There are positive and negative perceptions of every reality. The negative perception sees only the human tragedy. The positive sees the impulsive, instinctive, intuitive eruption of a caring and sharing spirit that occurs because of the tragedy. This explains why, in the darkest hour, this scenario unfolds time after time:

Catastrophe strikes!
The news is confirmed and reported.
Compassionate friends appear from everywhere and seemingly nowhere.
They huddle with the hurting heart and cry together.
They take time to pray together, eat together, and—almost always—laugh together!

Yes! Laughter in the trenches! Laughter in the emergency room! Laughter in the living room, where family and friends have gathered for a wake. I have heard laughter at the reception of almost every funeral I have ever attended or presided over.

This laughter—is it irreverence? No! It is a natural expression of joy breaking forth after the dark gloom of tragedy has lifted. As the Bible says,

Weeping may endure for a night,
But joy comes in the morning (Ps. 30:5).

Recently on a TV talk show, the host asked me, "Are you always happy, Dr. Schuller? And how can you be happy when things are so bad?"

His question triggered a thought, an explanation that had never occurred to me before. It amazed me, for in it I saw a basis for understanding the psychological and spiritual reactions we have to our world around us. This was the answer I gave my host: "I can be happy because *it's not the reality that is important— it's my perception of the reality that really matters. I can be happy no matter what happens to me, if I can maintain a positive perception of that reality.*"

Many of you women who have been hit with the reality of

breast cancer know what I'm talking about. My wife Arvella knows, too, because she has not been spared from this disease. When she was diagnosed as having a malignancy of the breast with surgery required, she had to decide how she would perceive this reality.

One of her perceptions of her very real breast cancer could have been, "Oh, this is going to devastate me. I will no longer be attractive to my husband. I'll probably get cancer in some other part of my body in a few years and die." If Arvella had adopted that reaction, she would have lost hope, and even if she lives a long life, it would be a life filled with fear and pain. This would be a negative perception of a reality.

Mercifully, this was *not* the reaction Arvella chose. She chose to believe she could conquer cancer. She chose to believe she could be whole and well again despite her mastectomy. And she is alive and happy and very, very busy in the ministry of the "Hour of Power."

When your perception of reality is positive, you can be happy, no matter what happens. If today you have no money, if you're poverty-stricken or on the verge of bankruptcy, you need to examine your perception of this condition. On the one hand, you can decide this is a total tragedy—you're wiped out, you're finished. On the other hand, you can look upon this as an opportunity to make some much-needed changes.

When you change your thinking, when you develop a positive perception, an amazing thing happens. Suddenly the reality is no longer as disastrous. After all it's not a disaster unless you *think* it's disastrous.

If you will perceive your problem as a possibility in disguise, then a stumbling block can become a steppingstone. The obstacle will now, be an opportunity. The problem is a challenge, and fatigue is replaced by a new rush of energy.

You can apply this principle to physical and economic conditions. It even works with personal relationships. Perhaps you have to work with or live with someone whom you can't handle. This person grates on your nerves.

I won't argue the point. But I will challenge your perception of what that reality means.

Negative perceptions block, obstruct your imagination from the positive possibilities. All you can see is the problem. You are blinded to the solutions, the possibilities for something even better. All you see is the hurt and the anger. You can't see the love and the joy that is hidden—waiting to be released.

On the other hand, a positive perception can unlock, reveal, release hidden possibilities. Suddenly you can see that life isn't so bad after all. Maybe things will work out. Maybe this is just God's way of guiding you. The positive perception looks for LOVE!

Where does this love come from? It comes from God Himself. Consequently, the deduction is clear: *If there's a lot of love in the world, there must be a lot of God in the world!*

So when I am asked, "How can you believe in God when all hell breaks loose?" I answer that question this way: "How dare I *not* believe in God when all hell breaks loose? I have enough problems without adding dangerous blinding doubt!"

Remember: God will allow nothing—and no one—to rob you of your option to react positively!

Faith then is the intelligent choice! Faith is the courageous choice! Jump onto the train. Choose to believe—in God—in a God of love!

BOARD THE TRAIN—CHOOSE TO LOVE GOD!

Several influences and misconceptions hold people back from loving God. As a pastor I have heard and seen these time and again, and I must say that most of the hindrances were

Crystal Cathedral Prayer

Lord,
Make my life
A window
For Your light
To shine through

And a mirror
To reflect Your love
To every person I meet.

subliminal. The people were unaware of what was keeping them from a loving relationship with God.

More often than not, people are unable to love God because they suffer from negative perceptions of God. Are you having trouble loving God? If your perception of your Creator is negative, then you must ask yourself some crucial questions.

To What Extent Is My Negative Perception of God a Result of My Negative Perception of Myself?

Emotional pollutants can distort our perceptions of God. These pollutants are guilt and shame and lack of self-esteem.

Remember: *Perception is a mirror.* Perhaps you have not visited Junction One—"Love Yourself and Be Happy!" You are not adequately loving yourself and are therefore crippling your ability to appreciate and love God.

When people say to me, "Oh, Dr. Schuller, you're such a beautiful person," I chuckle and answer them this way: "Wait a minute. That is only your perception of me. Perception is not a window; perception is a mirror. If you see beauty in me, you are seeing your own beauty in me. It takes one to know one!"

"Beautiful" people are quick to spot "beautiful" traits in somebody else. The opposite is true as well. When you see something unattractive in somebody's life, perhaps it bothers you so much because that same quality exists within you. *Perception is a mirror.*

How you see God will depend a great deal on how you perceive yourself. Angry people either don't believe in God or believe in an angry God. On the other hand, loving people believe in God and believe in a loving God.

To What Extent Is My Negative Perception of God a Result of My Ancestry?

Was your negative perception of God born in your family? Did your parents have (1) no faith at all or (2) a very negative and destructive faith? You probably need to know that embracing a faith that appears to violate your inheritance of knowledge and understanding will not be easy.

Most of us live with the tension of the pull of tomorrow and the tug of yesterday. To what extent are we responsible to carry on the lives of our ancestors? To pursue their projects? To fight their wars? To nurture their life's work? To propagate their doubts, their unbeliefs, their negative perceptions of God?

Tradition and perpetuity have validity only if they protect and advance truth. You may say, "I don't think I could become a believer or a Christian because my parents were not. And I wouldn't want to offend them or embarrass them, even if they are dead!"

Then I must ask you this question: "Do you not honor your parents if you improve on their beliefs? If you left a flawed inheritance to your children, would you not feel honored to see them lovingly correct your imperfect work?"

Dare we modify our parental heritage? Many of us don't, but if we improve our parents' perceptions, prejudices, ignorances, or inaccuracies, do we not improve our ongoing family history?

We have to understand this because it helps us understand some of the reasons why the wars keep going on in Northern Ireland and in the Middle East. It may be what keeps us from loving God, too.

Positivize your perceptions of God. Don't miss out on faith just to be faithful to family history and traditions!

To What Extent Is My Negative Perception of God a Result of My Spiritual Habitat?

If we have negative perceptions of God, it could be because we human beings are out of our natural habitat.

Mountains are hidden by the fog. But that doesn't mean that the peaks are not there. The sun is often shadowed by the clouds, but that doesn't mean it isn't shining. Likewise, our perceptions of God may be tainted by emotional pollutants in our spiritual environment; but that doesn't mean God does not exist or that He doesn't care.

Do you realize how much your spiritual environment is affected by your physical surroundings? Have you stopped to think why it's often more difficult to find God in crowded cities than in the peaceful countryside?

I first learned of the great impact our physical surroundings have on our spiritual environment when I was introduced to Neutra's theory of bio-realism. Richard Neutra was, of course, a great architect who designed buildings in coordination with the landscape in order to create environments that were conducive to positive emotions. Neutra taught that when you take human beings out of their natural habitat, surround them daily with concrete and steel, and bombard them with the noise of traffic, the silver voice of God is drowned out.

Neutra's theory is substantiated when I meet people who say, "Reverend, I must tell you honestly—frequently, I feel closer to God on the golf course than I do in church."

There is some truth to that statement. That's why I contracted Neutra to design our walk-in, drive-in church where the sounds and sights of moving traffic are eliminated from the senses and replaced by views of tranquil garden settings. In effect, through architecture, human beings in such a building are brought back to the environment for which they were created. It is an environment that lifts the fog and allows the spirit within man to feel and to hear God clearly, free from the environmental pollutants.

These are some of the causes of negative perceptions of God. If you suffer from any of them, it's important to understand that they are *miss*-conceptions: If you allow them to affect your relationship with God, you'll *miss* love! You'll *miss* life! You'll *miss* laughter! You'll *miss* joy!

On the other hand, the positive conceptions of God are the *true*-conceptions. The truth is that: God *is* Love! God's love *is* unconditional! God's love *is* non-judgmental!

Are you still skeptical? Let's spend just a little more time at Junction Two!

GOD DOES NOT SAY, "I'LL LOVE YOU *IF* . . ."

On Sundays in the Crystal Cathedral we stop during the service and ask those present to say to at least one other person, "God loves you and so do I!" We don't say, "God will love you *if* you are good and worthy of His love." We don't say, "God will love you *if* you can perfectly follow the Ten Commandments." We don't say, "God will love you *if* you will come to church every Sunday."

No! We don't have to prove ourselves to win the love and approval of God the Heavenly Father. His love and grace and eternal life are not prizes that we need to qualify for or promotions that need to be earned.

We have all heard the story of Pinocchio. Geppetto, the kind wood carver, longed for a son of his own. One day he "wished upon a star" and asked that the puppet he had made, Pinocchio, be turned into a real boy.

That night, as Geppetto slept, a fairy came and brought

Pinocchio partially to life. He was able to walk and talk without any strings. But he was still made of wood. She promised him that if he could prove that he was a good boy, she would return and make him into a *real* boy.

That's not how it is with God. We don't have to earn our love from Him. We don't have to prove ourselves to Him. He does not say, "I'll love you *if* you'll live an exemplary life." He loves us exactly as we are—right now!

One of the most well-known Bible verses is John 3:16: "For God so loved the world that He gave His only begotten Son, that whoever believes in Him should not perish but have everlasting life."

Notice that this verse does not say, "God so loved nice, good, perfect, holy people."

No! It says, "God so loved the *world*!" That means that He came, He lived, He loved—for *all*! J. Wallace Hamilton once said, "Jesus Christ is walking the highways of life looking for the riffraff, looking for the sinners like you and me—hounding us until He catches us, not to point an accusing finger, but to remind us who we are—children of God, for whom He died, whom God wants to use as His princes and princesses in His kingdom."

GOD DOES NOT SAY, "I'LL LOVE YOU *WHEN* . . ."

God doesn't wait for you to love Him. He loves you now! He doesn't say, "I'll love you *when* you love me!" No—aware that you may flee from His love—He still makes the plunge; He makes the commitment; He makes the decision to love you.

Thank heaven that God decided to become involved with you and with me anyway! The act of sending Jesus to earth, the Incarnation, was only one of the decisions God made. Before that God decided to create human beings—people with the freedom to choose or not to choose, to reject or to accept, to run to love or to retreat from love. God made the human being a most unique creature.

Then, when we messed up the creation and allowed sin and negative forces to enter in, God made the decision to correct the situation by sending His Son to teach us the truth about living. This son, Jesus, not only told us the truth, He lived the truth. He was as He said, "the way, the truth, and the life."

God made the decision to send Christ to this world to save us knowing that it would cost Him the life of His one and only Son. He made the decision knowing that many would turn their backs on the love and the life He was offering them. But He didn't wait for us to ask Him to do it. Knowing full well that many would never accept it, He decided to give His Son's life *before* we knew we needed it.

GOD DOES NOT SAY, "I'LL LOVE YOU *BUT . . .*"

God doesn't say, "I'll love you, *but* you must earn it."

This is an extremely difficult concept for most of us to accept. After all, as children we were taught to obey the rules. Our parents, whether they meant to or not, frequently conveyed the idea that their love had to be earned. When we were bad, their love was withheld. Even the best of parents are guilty of this tactic at one time or another, for certainly who among us can mask our disappointments and frustrations when our children fail to live up to our expectations for them? That doesn't mean we love them less; however, that is the message that children frequently receive.

There is a beautiful word in the Bible: *Grace*.

"What does that word really mean?" I asked my seminary

professor, Dr. Simon Blocker. I'll never forget his answer. It was so sound, psychologically and religiously!

"Grace," he answered, "is God's love in action for those who don't deserve it."

Grace is a gift. It can't be bought. It can't be earned. It is freely given. But a gift isn't really a gift until it is accepted! God offers to *all* the gift of grace. He offers the gift of love, the gift of a new you. Can you think of a better gift?

God's beautifully wrapped gift of grace came just in time for a woman I know named Sherrie. During the turbulent sixties she was a college student at Berkeley where she had begun using LSD. When her parents asked her to come home for a visit, Sherrie agreed, with one provision—that she would be able to return to Berkeley and never come home again. I received a telephone call from her parents urging me to talk with her while she was home.

The entire family came to my office together—father, mother, and daughter. Sherrie looked terrible. Her beautiful young face was distorted. Inner tensions, guilt, and her hardened attitude had altered her appearance. With sincerity she declared to me, "I have found God in LSD. Every Friday night we have our services. It's beautiful. You don't know what God is like until you've found God in LSD."

"I believe I have found God in Jesus Christ," I replied. "You claim," I continued, "that you have found God in LSD. Who's right? You or me? Let's put God to the test."

She nodded her head approvingly.

"God is love—do you agree?"

She said she did.

"Love is helping people," I added. "Do you agree?"

She nodded her head again.

"How much money have you collected in your LSD services to feed the hungry, to help the crippled, to find a cure for cancer?" I asked.

She was silent.

"I must tell you, Sherrie," I went on, "because of the Spirit of Jesus Christ that lives in the people in this church, we have been able to convert thousands of dollars over the past twelve months into help for human beings with problems. The Christian church has built hospitals and institutions to treat the blind, the sick, and the lame and has provided care for millions of unhappy people."

A sad look of disillusionment began to appear on Sherrie's face.

"Let's all stand, hold hands, and pray," I suggested. Father, mother, daughter, and I joined hands in a circle. I offered this simple prayer. "Jesus Christ, Your Spirit of Love lives within my heart. I pray that You will come into the life and heart of this beautiful young woman."

As I finished, I saw a tear slide from her eye. I reached over with my finger and picked up the wet drop of warm emotion from her soft cheek. Holding it before her, I exclaimed, "Sherrie! Look what fell out of your eye! Didn't you feel beautiful inside when this tear was forming and falling? This is the deepest and most joyous experience a human being can know. It is religious emotion. It is the movement of the divine Spirit within you. Christ is coming into your life, Sherrie. Let Him come in. Don't be afraid of Him. Nothing good ever dies inside when Christ comes in.

"Look at the sky—it is blue. Look at the grass—it is really green. Look at the flowers—they are really red. While you had this high trip, which put this beautiful tear in your eye, you were not in complete control of yourself. This is reality. It is not artificially induced. It is authentic. The world around you is not distorted or hidden in a psychedelic fog. You can trust this Christ." At that point tears were flowing freely from Sherrie's eyes. She felt the love of God for her.

Almost immediately her facial expression changed. The

narrowing eyes of suspicion and rebellion changed into the round, open, beautiful eyes of wonderment. The face, which had been tight, tense, and older than her years, relaxed. Once more the cheeks had the full blossom and the warm, rounded shape of a pretty young maiden.

As I write this, Sherrie is now a beautiful young wife and mother. She has devoted much of her life to helping others discover the supreme joy of knowing Jesus Christ.

The Love of God—it is there, a priceless gift, for you and for me. He doesn't say, "You can be saved, but you'll have to earn it." He doesn't say, "You can have my love, but you'll have to pay me for it." No! He only says, "You are loved! My love is a gift! Pure and simple; free and clear; no down payment necessary!"

John Newton said it years ago. Singers still sing the timeless words today:

> Amazing grace, how sweet the sound
> That saved a wretch like me!
> I once was lost, but now am found,
> Was blind, but now I see.

GOD DOESN'T SAY, "I'LL LOVE YOU *AFTER . . .*"

God doesn't say, "I'll love you *after* you see the error of your ways, *after* you come back to me on your hands and knees." No! He goes out looking for you. You are His creation. He made you. He loves you. He wants to welcome you as His child into His arms.

You may remember the traditional story of Helen of Troy. There is an alternative legend in which this beautiful queen was captured and carried away and became a victim of amnesia. She became a prostitute in the streets. She didn't know her name or the fact that she came from royal blood. But, back in her homeland, friends didn't give up. One Greek man believed she was alive and went to look for her. He never lost faith.

One day while wandering through the streets, he came to a waterfront and saw a wretched woman in tattered clothes with deep lines across her face. There was something about her that seemed familiar so he walked up to her and asked, "What is your name?" She gave a name that was meaningless to him. "May I see your hands?" he pursued because he knew the lines in Helen's hands. She held her hands out in front of her, and the young man gasped, "You are Helen! You are Helen of Troy! Don't you remember?"

She looked up at him in astonishment.

"Helen of Troy!" he repeated. The fog began to clear. There was recognition in her face. The light came on! She discovered her lost self! She put her arms around her old friend and wept. She discarded the tattered clothes and once more became the queen she was born to be!

God searches for you in the same way. He uses every method possible to look for you and try to convince you of your worth to Him.

GOD DOES NOT SAY, "I'LL LOVE YOU *THEREFORE* . . ."

God doesn't say, "I love you . . . *therefore* you are favored in my sight and will never suffer; never hurt; never experience pain, rejection, setbacks, or grief!"

Unreasonable, confused expectations, more than anything else, can rupture relationships. If you expect that because God loves you, *therefore* you should never experience heartbreak, your expectation is unrealistic and your relationship with God will turn sour. The truth is—God will give you grace to become a more beautiful and loving human being if you keep trusting Him through tragedy.

"You always seem so happy," I said to my dear friend, Art Linkletter. "I remember when your daughter, Diane, committed suicide at the age of seventeen. Then, I remember not too many years ago when your thirty-one-year-old son was instantly killed in an auto accident. I don't know how often you and I have been together since those two tragedies, but I always experience powerful vibrations of joy in your presence. Explain it to me. How can I interpret this to my readers? I'm totally convinced you're not a phony. I know you are a sincerely happy man."

"Oh yes, Bob," Art replied with that great, happy grin of his. "I've never been happier anytime in my life than I am today. I can't go anywhere without somebody approaching me and telling me of their pain. And I find my joy in comforting them. There's no doubt about it; I am a more compassionate human being. The loss of my children makes me want to love everybody, and that's what makes me happy!"

GOD DOES SAY, *"I LOVE YOU"*—PERIOD!—EXCLAMATION POINT!

Love? It's there! It's unconditional! It's free, no strings attached! But you'll never be able to know it or see it or feel it until you come to terms with your Creator. He created love. He is the Source of love. And you will not be able to grow in your love for yourself or for others until you reach out and accept His love, until you can say "God loves me! This I know!"

If you have trouble believing that you are loved by God, if it is hard for you to see how much you mean to Him, then maybe this story will help.

Once there was a little boy who made a sailboat. He carefully carved the hull from wood, then lovingly sanded it smooth and delicately brushed on the paint. Next he cut the sail from the whitest cloth. When he finished it he couldn't wait to see if his boat was "seaworthy," so he took it to the lake. He found a grassy spot by the edge of the water, knelt down, and gently set the boat on the water. Then he blew a little puff of air and waited.

The boat didn't move, so he blew a little harder until a breeze filled the tiny sail and the boat pulled away from the shore. "It sails! It sails!" he cried out, clapping his hands and dancing along the side of the lake. But then he stopped. He realized he had not tied a string to the boat. He watched as his creation moved farther and farther away until it was out of his reach.

The little boy was both happy and sad—thrilled that his boat had sailed, but saddened because it was now out of his reach. He ran home crying.

Sometime later the boy was wandering through town when he passed a toy shop that sold both new and old toys. There in the window was his boat! He was ecstatic. He ran in and said happily to the shopkeeper, "That's my boat! That's my boat!"

The man looked down at the little boy and said, "I'm sorry. I bought the boat. It is for sale, though."

"But it's my boat," the boy cried out. "I made it! I sailed it! I lost it! It's mine!"

"I'm sorry," the shopkeeper said again. "If you want it you will have to pay for it."

"How much is it?" the lad asked. When he found out the price he was shattered. He had only a few coins in his bank at home. His head drooping, he left the store.

But this little boy was very determined. When he got home he went to his room and counted his pennies, nickels, dimes, and quarters to find out how much more money he would need before he could buy back his precious boat. So he worked and

**Grace
is
God's love
in action
for
those
who don't
deserve it!**

saved until finally he had just the right amount. He ran back to the store, hoping the boat would still be there. He laughed with joy; there it was sitting in the window just as before.

He ran into the shop, dug into his pockets, and placed all of his money on the counter. "I want to buy my boat!" he exclaimed.

The shopkeeper lifted the little sailboat out of the window and placed it in the excited boy's hands. The boy grasped the boat tightly to his chest and ran home proudly, saying, "You *are* my boat. You *are* my boat! You're *twice* my boat! First, you're my boat because I made you, and second, you're my boat because I bought you!"

If you were that boat you would know that you were loved. The news I have for you, my friend, is this: You are that sailboat! Jesus Christ is the little boy. And the cross is the price! You are God's child twice over. First, you were God's child because He made you. Second, you are God's child because He bought you on the cross of Calvary, and He will go to all lengths to get you back!

One of my favorite illustrations of this unconditional redemptive love of God is the musical drama *The Man of La Mancha.* In the musical, Don Quixote meets a woman of the streets, a wild, wanton wench named Aldonza. The man of La Mancha stops short, looks at her intently, and announces that she is his lady. He will call her "Dulcinea." She responds, with mocking laughter, that she is hardly a lady.

Still Don Quixote sees the seed of potential greatness and tries desperately to give her a new self-image of the person she really is—if she can believe it. He *insists* that she is his lady.

Angered and hurt, with wild hair flying over nearly naked breasts, she screams that she is only a kitchen maid! She is *Aldonza,* not Dulcinea!

She runs from the stage as the man of La Mancha whispers again and again that she is his lady. At the close of the play Don

Quixote is dying. He feels he has failed. The good he has tried to give has been rejected. The love he has offered has been shunned. But, then to his side comes a "born-again" Aldonza. She is now lovely with a new gentleness. Confused, he does not recognize this lovely stranger until in a warm voice she tells him that she is his Dulcinea. She has been saved from self-hate and has been taught self-love.

God's love is like the man of La Mancha's! He sees you *not* as you are, but as you can *become*! He sees the lady in *every* woman! The gentleman in *every* male! He sees you as the gentle, caring person who is loved and who can love in return! He sees the beauty in you—and will help you become the person He wants you to be.

Now then, it is possible to believe in a God of love! And when you see all that He has done, don't you think He deserves to be loved by you?

Don't pass by this all-important junction on this journey of love! Choose to believe in God! Choose to love God—and *be happy*!

JUNCTION THREE:
LOVE OTHERS— AND BE HAPPY!

A conductor of the train at Disneyland has made the loop hundreds, perhaps thousands, of times. He has watched the people wait eagerly for the approaching train. He has seen them surge happily through the gates in response to the call, "All Aboard!"

In contrast, when we are invited to take the trip on the Happy Railroad's train of love, most of us hold back. We may approach the junctions hesitantly, suspiciously. Some of us turn and run away.

Why is that? If love is so beautiful, so profoundly satisfying, so happiness-producing, why doesn't every normal human being instinctively, intuitively, irresistibly race to embrace fellow humans with a holy hug? Why don't we rush headlong into happy relationships? Could it be that we're afraid to get on board at "Love Your Neighbor and Be Happy!"—afraid of rejection? Of failure? Of involvement? Of oppression?

And what is fear? It is simply a lack of faith.

DON'T HOLD BACK! ONLY BELIEVERS CAN BE LOVERS!

Possibility thinkers are people of faith who dare to believe that anything is possible. They dare to run risks! They have the faith to love, and that's important because *only believers can be lovers.*

Another question comes to mind. If lack of love is fear, and if the presence of fear is lack of faith, then why do we lack the faith to plunge into a life controlled by love?

One of the reasons—shockingly—is that some people have *never* experienced healthy, honest love! It's painful to face up to—but it does happen. There are people who have gone through an entire life and have *never* known love. Perhaps their birth was the result of a night of passion between a man and a woman. So they never were truly welcomed and loved in birth or childhood or in their teen-age or young adult years.

Widespread child abuse is the most tragic reason why some are afraid of love. Social institutions, meanwhile, have often failed as well. Educational, political, even religious institutions have established priorities and prejudices that leave little or no time for ebullient, effervescent expressions of affection. So some people lack the faith to love because the concept is totally foreign to their perception of reality!

No wonder many, if not most, living human beings cry out, "Yes, Dr. Schuller, love may make you happy, and that's why I'm unhappy—*nobody* loves me!"

I dare you to have the faith to believe that there are in this world people who are trying to reach you, to love you. They honestly and deeply care about you more than you could ever know. There are fellowship groups, intimate colonies of caring Christians, scattered around this world.

You tried and were hurt? Disillusioned? Try again! And the fact that you have never experienced love doesn't mean you can discount its reality.

Remember this: Never judge reality by your *limited* experience. I have never been to Mt. Everest, yet I believe it is there! I trust the verified reports of those who have climbed its icy, rocky face. As you believe in the seas even if you have not sailed them, so you can believe in love, even if you have never experienced it.

In other cases faith in love has been shattered by crude encounters with counterfeit love. Tragic stories can be told of the innocent lover who has been exploited, manipulated, used, ripped off, and left lonely, bleeding, shocked, bitter! More often than not, this person was a victim of a love that was a selfish "I need you" or "I want you" display of passion.

If the only encounter a person has with love is a "commercial," interpersonal relationship, where love is only given to get something in return, then of course it would be difficult to acquire the faith to love.

Or if "getting love" or "being loved" always has a "price tag," this is judgmental "love."

- The teacher "loves" me when I do a good job!
- My parents "love" me when I obey.
- My religious authorities and God (as I interpret Him) "love" me when I live by the rules.

Love, at this point, has become a reward to be handed out! And withholding of love becomes a silent and cruel form of punishment! No wonder many persons yield to a natural inclination to shyness. A fear of intimacy takes over. People take the attitude that sex may be O.K. but intimacy is out! So they choose to "make love" without revealing their names.

Such an attempt to protect ourselves is terribly dangerous. A cold, hard shell will inadvertently be built around the heart and soul. The result: A deep-seated fear of loving. Love and happiness are lost.

If we are asked, *"What, then, is real love?"* we could offer one of these three answers:

1. "I love you because I need you."

Love relationships do fill mutual needs—and that's O.K! But if love rises no higher than this "I need you" level, it is, indeed, basically selfish. The dangers of selfish love are obvious: This path leads to jealousy and extreme possessiveness. Fear is the end result—the fear of losing a prized possession!

2. "I love you because I want you."

Passion does have a proper place in all healthy love relationships. But passion alone can be sheer lust. This path too will generate enormous negative tension. Passion does not deserve all the credit that it has been given by romance novelists and soap operas. Passion is *not* proof of love, anymore than lack of passion is absence of love. So let us not be deceived. Let us see real love as it is. As the poet William Blake wrote:

> This life's dim windows of the soul
> Distorts the heavens from pole to pole
> And leads us to believe a lie
> When you see with, not through, the eye.

I am reminded of a man who is unmarried. He is in his fifties, and he was despairing to me recently because his life is lonely; he has never had a family. "The trouble is," he said, "I once knew a young girl, but there wasn't the passion for her that I thought should have been there. So I foolishly thought I didn't love her. However, I deeply respected and trusted her! Now, in retrospect, I see that this was love, but I didn't know it. So I let love pass me by."

How often have we passed love by because we have not recognized it for what it is?

3. "I love you because you need me."

This is REAL love! This is the love that releases the hidden possibilities. This love wipes out fear—FOREVER!

Why does real love cast out fear? For one simple reason: Real love is a self-*less* love. Self-*ish* love always produces fear. If I love you only because I *need you,* or if I love you only because I *want you,* I'm going to be afraid that I might not win you or hold you. So I'll live in the fearful anxiety of losing you.

But! If I love because I want to give something to you, I'll never be fearful or worried or tense, *for a giving love can never lose!*

Give love, and if it's accepted, you have succeeded! If love is rejected, you still have your love to give to someone else who is waiting to accept and appreciate it!

WHY SHOULD I RUSH TO BOARD THE LOVE TRAIN?

There are two very good reasons to rush to love. The first is that *real love releases my hidden possibilities!*

Although love can hurt, although love can bring disappointment, pain, and rejection—*real* love also brings with it *possibilities!* As Amanda McBroom says so beautifully in her song, "The Rose":

Some say love, it is a river that drowns the tender reed.
Some say love, it is a razor that leaves your heart to bleed.
Some say love, it is a hunger, an endless, aching need;
I say love it is a flower, and you its only seed.

It's the heart afraid of breaking, that never learns to dance.
It's the dream afraid of waking, that never takes the chance.
It's the one who won't be taken, who cannot seem to give;
And the soul afraid of dying, that never learns to live.

When the night has been too lonely,
And the road has been too long,
And you think that love is only for the lucky and the strong,
Just remember, in the winter, far beneath the bitter snows,
Lies the seed that with the sun's love,
In the spring, becomes the rose. *

We should rush to get on the Love Train because we all long to bloom like the rose. We must be willing to take the chance that, in spite of the challenges and risks, we will discover the real love that can melt the snows and wake the slumbering possibilities swelling within us.

With the warmth of real love, confidence is born within me. I feel loved, and I project that love to others. In the process this love becomes a magnet. It attracts happy and creative people who bring with them inspiring ideas, and in their presence we find inspiration, enlightenment, insight! We are left with an expanded imagination! Latent possibilities emerge in our thinking!

We rush to love because it draws us to new people who stimulate our settled minds with new ideas. Suddenly our minds are opened to fresh possibilities. We discover new doors opening to new relationships! Eye-opening insights! Even faith in God! In ourselves! And in others! So, in the presence of love, the creative process proceeds. "Impossible" situations become challenges that beckon as great possibilities!

The second reason we rush to get on the love train is that *real love releases and encourages the greatness that we all have within.*

We all want to be great at something! Whether it be a great husband, wife, parent, employee, or employer, none of us *really* wants to be mediocre. And nothing releases greatness within people more than love.

You may remember seeing Ed Burke carry the American flag and lead America's Olympians into the Los Angeles Coliseum for the 1984 Olympiad. Ed Burke is a great hammer thrower, a great husband, and a great father. What you may not know is that Ed's greatness, as well as the fact that he was in the coliseum that day carrying the flag, is a result of the loving support of his wife, Shirley.

Ed told me after the Olympics, "Dr. Schuller, Shirley and I carried that flag in *together,* and I believe the fact that I was chosen to carry the flag validated what we have done together, which is a lot of very hard work, inspiration on her part, help in coaching, and a marriage commitment for over twenty-five years. I think the Olympic Committee wanted to tell America that it's possible! 'This couple did it.' That's why I say that she was with me every step of the way."

Shirley's support of her husband has been extraordinary, to say the least. In 1961, Ed and his bride were students at San Jose State where Ed was a young hammer thrower, the best collegiate thrower in the country. One day he asked Shirley to come watch him throw for the newspapers and be interviewed. A newspaper photographer wanted one more picture. Ed threw the hammer. It was a very good throw. Ed was performing better than ever before.

The photographer left. Since it was cold, Shirley walked to the car. Ed wanted to make one more throw, but this one went completely out of control. The hammer ripped from his grasp and careened one hundred feet into the automobile where Shirley was sitting. The hammer struck her in the head with full force.

Ed thought he had killed her. It was the most tragic moment in his life. He drove his unconscious wife to the hospital.

Although Shirley regained consciousness and suffered no long-term side effects from the injury, Ed was devastated. He felt he could never throw the hammer again.

But, Shirley believed in him! She loved him! She saw the possibilities in him. She knew that he had promise. He was going to be a good hammer thrower. In order to get him back on the field, she coached and worked with him herself. The two of them worked together so successfully that Ed was actually able to enter the 1964 Olympic games. Shirley then coached Ed through the American record and the longest throw in the world in 1967.

The Burkes continued to work together until the 1968 Olympics in Mexico City. At that event, however, Ed became disenchanted with the program because of the political upheaval among the athletes. So he quit. Ed became a good businessman, a good teacher, a wonderful father, but that was not enough for Ed. Eleven years later, as Ed was turning 40, Shirley could see that he was becoming more and more restless.

One day, while watching the world games on television, Shirley saw some Russian hammer throwers. Shirley noticed that they weren't very big men. This was intriguing because experts believed that an athlete would have to be bigger and bigger to be able to throw farther and farther. But the Russians had found a new way of throwing that was more fitted to a smaller man.

Shirley called Ed to the television. Their daughters watched as well. They had never seen their father throw the hammer, and they begged him to throw the hammer for them. Ed said, "No!" But the girls found an old rusty hammer in the garage, took sandpaper and SOS pads and cleaned it up, and again begged their dad to show them.

This time Ed could not refuse. He took his family in a truck to a large field at San Jose State. He threw once, twice, and again. The neuromuscular patterns were still there. Ed threw ten times before he was ready to go home. A vision of himself walking into the Los Angeles Coliseum for the next Olympics came clearly to him. He had marched twice before in the middle of the Olympic parade and remembered how wonderful it was to represent his nation. He turned and looked at Shirley. As if she read his mind, she said with a smile, *I know*!

Once again Ed and Shirley Burke embarked on a training schedule. Here was a man in his forties challenging young men half his age. But once he made his intentions known, many other men his age and older throughout the world contacted him. He became their champion.

Of course he made the team and was selected by the American team's twenty-two captains to carry the American flag in the opening ceremony. Shirley and Ed talked about how he should hold the flag—high! For two reasons: First, because he wanted to present his country's flag as high as he could; and secondly, because he wanted to hold it up high to the heavens, thanking God and praising God every step of the way.

The great day came, and when Ed entered the Coliseum he was floating. The music and the roar of the crowd held him up. Shirley, who was watching from the sixth row, slipped out of her seat and maneuvered her way to the side of the track. As Ed came by, with all the love and pride she could muster, she shouted, "Hold it higher!"

Ed admits that his wife's love brought him out of self-imposed, fear-induced, guilt-inspired retirement to take the path that led to his glorious moment!

HERE'S A TRIP THAT WILL TRANSFORM YOUR LIFE!

The junction, "Love Your Neighbor and Be Happy!" attracts a variety of passengers.

People who choose to love people really change! No wonder they discover real happiness! Some who board at this stop are "I-I" people. Others are "I-It" people. What a happy change awaits both of them!

"I-I" People

The "I-I" person tries to find emotional fulfillment in feeding an insecure ego, satisfying selfish pleasures, and making sure he gets his own way. When faced with decisions, this kind of person asks questions like:

- "What's in it for me?"
- "What will I get out of it?"
- "Does it fit in with my plans?"

It does not matter if others like it; it does not matter that others could be helped; it does not matter that others are hurting.

This is the nonsharing, noncaring, no-burden-bearing person. Someone is crying? Someone is dying? Tough! Rough! "I've enough problems of my own" is the answer this person gives. Instead of, "Oh! Let me help you!"

There is a great deal of evidence to indicate that by nature most people tend to be "I-I" persons.

A person's entire character is affected by the "I-I" attitude.

The "I-I" attitude affects the value system. "I want what I want when I want it the way I want it" sums up the value system in one selfish sentence. "Do your own thing, I'll do mine" is another expression.

The "I-I" attitude molds the emotional life. Such self-centered people soon discover that very few people sincerely care for them. Hence, they become insecure, defensive, oppressive, suspicious, and cynical. They yield to a frenetic pleasure drive

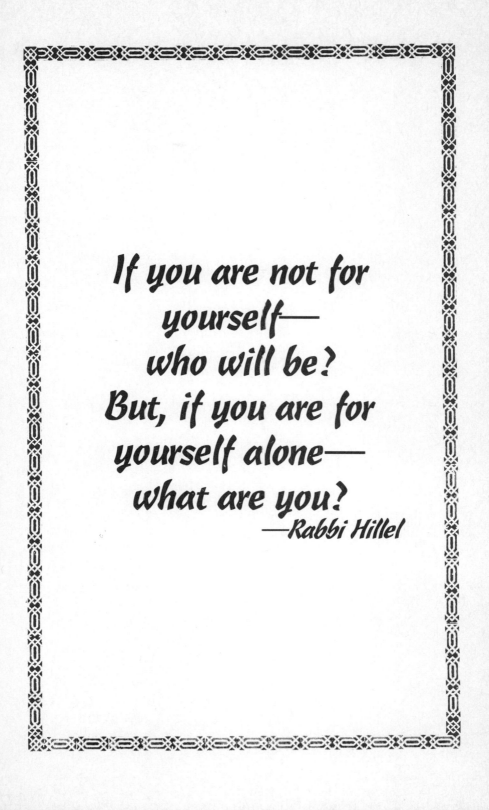

*If you are not for
yourself—
who will be?
But, if you are for
yourself alone—
what are you?*
        —Rabbi Hillel

in a neurotic effort to escape from facing a self they are not proud of. Or they drive themselves toward more power, foolishly believing that power and position will make people look up to them. They mistakenly think that they will then truly respect themselves as well. Too late, sometimes never, these people learn that the "I-I" route never builds self-respect.

The "I-I" person cannot give—so he cannot accept. For accepting always requires giving. You have to give your honest, humble attention to accept advice, criticism, and suggestions. You have to give a heartfelt concern before you can accept the burdens of others and be able to say, "I care about you." You have to give your freedom before you can accept involvement in worthy causes. You have to give your time, talent, and treasure before you can really accept responsibility.

One of the greatest lessons we must learn today is that humanity is an organismic unity. We are all in the same boat on planet Earth. What hurts others will ultimately hurt us. All people are closely linked on the spacecraft on which we live. An explosion occurs and you hear the bad news and see it on TV. It will distress, anger, worry, or frighten you. It is affecting you! You may eat and be merry, but you'll hear people who will talk about the terrible things that are happening.

Mass communication has helped make humankind realize that the world is also an emotionally organismic unity, like it or not! NO MAN IS AN ISLAND! We all have to live together. And really, it's for our own good that we do. Consider if we could be true, pure isolationists; if we never needed to interact with our neighbors, would we then be happy? No! For then we would be "I-I" people and "I-I" people can never be happy! Why? Because they miss out on real love!

"I-It" People

"I-It" persons relate primarily to things. They try to find emotional fulfillment in material acquisitions.

- Want joy? Get something new.
- Bored? Go shopping.
- Guilty? Buy a gift.
- Fearful? Buy a gun.
- Insecure? Build a bigger savings account.
- Need to impress people? Cars. Clubs. Cocktails will do it.
- Lonely? Go to a movie, a bar, or a motel.

To such individuals, even people become things, not persons with hopes, feelings, or dreams. People are toys to be played with, tools to use, trinkets for amusement, treasures to buy, or trash to be thrown away. Here's what happens to the person with an "I-It" outlook:

The "I-It" person is never emotionally satisfied or fulfilled. When things rust out, wear out, wrinkle, grow old, or go out of style, this individual never discovers that things do not feed self-respect or self-esteem on any lasting basis.

The "I-It" attitude also determines the value system. What's the salary? What are the fringe benefits? How much will it cost? These are *the* important questions.

The "I-It" person is never truly free, but is forever trapped by the tyranny of things. "Paint me. Paper me. Patch me. Repair me. Replace me," these things shout!

The "I-It" person never really loves. "I love you because I *want* you" or "I love you because I *need* you" is the limited depth of the love relationship of the "I-It" person. Other people are not known on a deep level; life is shallow, ultimately meaningless.

If "I-I" people and "I-It" people want to find love and to be happy, they'll have to become "I-You" people.

"I-You" People

"I-You" people have chosen to love their neighbors. They see people as persons who have dreams, desires, hurts, and needs. When an "I-I" person or an "I-It" person becomes an "I-You" person, what a change takes place:

The housewife becomes a homemaker!
The sire becomes a father!
The lover becomes a husband!
The lawyer becomes a counselor!
The teacher becomes a person builder!
The doctor becomes a healer!
The truck driver becomes a transporter of vital material!
The salesman becomes a supplier of human need!
The businessman becomes a job-opportunity creator!

One of the happiest and most well-loved men I have known was Theo Weaver. He was a friend for over thirty-five years, and the best neighbor anybody could ask for.

In 1955 when I came to California with my wife and $500 to start a church, Theo was the first man I met. At that time the church was only a dream. I met Theo at a restaurant. I told him who I was and why I had come to town. He agreed to help me. Sure enough, on that first Sunday, March 27, 1955, there he was handing out the printed programs and taking up the offering. He was our first usher. He went on to become a faithful member of the church board and stood by me, even when he didn't agree with me, through all the tough growing times in the church.

He was an "I-You" person, always willing to serve and put

others above himself. As I came to know Theo better, I learned how he gave of himself.

In addition to being a steadfast husband and father, he never missed a day and he was only *late* for work twice in the thirty years he worked for the Bell Telephone Company. When he died suddenly from a heart attack at the age of sixty, the Crystal Cathedral was filled with men who openly wept at the loss of this loving coworker. Widows whom he had helped by mowing their lawns grieved at the loss of their beloved neighbor. Opal, Sharla, and Glenn said goodbye reluctantly to their adored husband and father. I have officiated at thousands of funerals and memorial services in my life. Many of them have been for great statesmen, some have been for celebrities. None of these people was more *loved* than Theo.

His friend, Vernon Riphagen, wrote a poem when he heard of Theo's death. The family asked me to read it at his service. It summarizes the loving, happy life of a good friend and neighbor.

Our Father in Heaven we thank thee today
For having Theo Weaver pass by this way.
He would give of himself, he would give us his trust,
He'd go extra miles as all angels must.

A family man, husband, grandpa, and father,
His family was all, the worries didn't bother.
His friendship was deep, he was sincere
With all who knew him and held him so dear.

Loyal and faithful, employed by Bell
On Tuesday his heart wasn't working too well.
Then Wednesday his local life line was shattered.
He was plugged in to Heaven, and that's all that mattered.

We thank thee, Dear Lord, for caring for me
By sending such people as an example for me.

May we be as faithful, may we be true
When we make the long journey over to You. *

Theo was an "I-You" person, a loved person, a happy man. How do you become an "I-You" person? You become an "I-You" person by becoming an "I-*Him*" person.

What do I mean by "I-*Him*"? I believe Jesus Christ lived to show us true love! I believe He died to demonstrate true forgiving love. I believe He lives today, and I can pray to Him. He hears me! He cares about me. He loves me! I have a one-to-one relationship with Him. Now I have the courage to love others too!

In 1959 when we purchased the property on which the Crystal Cathedral stands today, I went to the post office and tried to get an address people could easily remember. "You'll need five numbers, Reverend Schuller," I was told.

"O.K., I'll take 1-1-1-1-1," I said.

"Sorry, the second number must be 2," the official declared.

"O.K., I'll take 1-2-3-4-5."

The man just laughed and shook his head, rejecting the idea outright.

"Well, then," I tried again, "1-2-2-2-2!"

Disgusted, he shot back at me—"No way! Now here is your address—take it or leave it—1-2-1-4-1!"

I left. Twenty years later I discovered the hidden, divine blessing. Why, the numbers said it all—what our joyous faith is all about: "one-to-One-for-one!" I relate to Jesus, so now I can relate to you! Of course! That translates "God loves you . . . and so do I!"

The invitation to be happy and loved was offered to everyone—everywhere—by Jesus Christ when he said, "You

---

*Used by permission.

shall love the LORD Your God . . . [and] *your neighbor as yourself*" (Mark 12:30–31). That invitation still stands today.

In this Bible verse, you have it: Three love opportunities open to you and every person! Three glorious possibilities to enter into a trusting and mutually affirming relationship: With yourself! With other human beings! With God!

Now, isn't that a trip that gets you excited and enthused? Then let's prepare for life's greatest journey by learning what "love" and "being loved" are all about.

Before you take your first trip to a strange place or a foreign country, you probably do what I do—get a guidebook and read up on the customs and culture. On the subject of love, the single most inspiring and illuminating guidebook ever written in any language is a chapter in the Holy Bible, 1 Corinthians 13. Let's look at it together: We'll learn lessons on love that will make our one trip on planet Earth a truly loving and happy venture!

. . . And
So
Do
I!

IF I SPEAK in the tongues of men and of angels, but have not love, I am a noisy gong or a clanging cymbal.

And if I have prophetic powers, and understand all mysteries and all knowledge, and if I have all faith, so as to remove mountains, but have not love, I am nothing.

If I give away all I have, and if I deliver my body to be burned, but have not love, I gain nothing.

Love is patient and kind; love is not jealous or boastful; it is not arrogant or rude. Love does not insist on its own way; it is not irritable or resentful; it does not rejoice at wrong, but rejoices in the right.

Love bears all things, believes all things, hopes all things, endures all things.

Love never ends; as for prophecies, they will pass away; as for tongues, they will cease; as for knowledge, it will pass away.

For our knowledge is imperfect and our prophecy is imperfect; but when the perfect comes, the imperfect will pass away.

When I was a child, I spoke like a child, I thought like a child, I reasoned like a child; when I became a man, I gave up childish ways.

For now we see in a mirror dimly, but then face to face. Now I know in part; then I shall understand fully, even as I have been fully understood.

So faith, hope, love abide, these three; but the greatest of these is love.

I Corinthians, Chapter 13

THE ROAD OF LOVE:
TAKE IT!
IT'S
THE *RIGHT*-WAY!

Love Is the Greatest

"The greatest of these is love."
1 Corinthians 13:13

"**G**od loves you . . . and so do I!" Two simple phrases. Alone each one is great—but together they combine to make a *life-transforming* prescription for joy!

In Part I, "God Loves You," you boarded the train, made the full loop, and saw how you can be happy and loved. Now get ready for the *real* journey! You can't stay in Disneyland forever! You need to get onto the road of life.

Now, the rugged, raw, real road of life is a far cry from Fantasyland. There are mountains that need to be climbed, rivers that must be crossed, bridges that will have to be built, walls that must be scaled.

The journey of life can be rough and it's easy to get lost, discouraged, and worn out. Personally, if I'm going to a great deal of effort to get somewhere, I like to check my location periodically and ask myself if I'm going the *right*-way. It doesn't do any good to keep going if you're on the *wrong* road or if you're going in the *wrong* direction on the *right* road.

So, on this journey of life, I ask myself two questions:

1. Am I on the right road?
2. Am I going in the right direction?

To help us navigate this challenging trip called life, God gave to us, through St. Paul, a road map. It's found in 1 Corinthians 13. This classic passage of Scripture clearly outlines for us how to find the right road and which direction to take.

AM I ON THE RIGHT ROAD?

You are on the right road—if you are on the road of love. Paul wrote ". . . *the greatest of these is love.*"

It sounds too simple, and it is so easy to get distracted and to think of the road to success, the road to faith, the road to riches as more important than plain old love.

A housewife and young mother named Ann woke up one day terribly depressed. She felt overwhelmed—by her children and by the schedules and demands that life heaped on her. It seemed that all she did was nag at her children. She barked at them and scolded them incessantly. When she stopped and looked at the mother she was portraying, she was a shrew. In the midst of her tears, she cried out to the Lord. Her answer came through the Bible: "If I speak in the tongues of men and of angels, but have not love, I am a noisy gong or a clanging cymbal. And if I have prophetic powers, and understand all mysteries and all knowledge . . . but have not love, I am nothing. If I give away all I have, and if I deliver my body to be burned, but have not love, I gain nothing" (1 Cor. 13:1–3).

Five words leaped out at this young mother, challenging her. She wrote them on her calendar. She posted them on her refrigerator. She taped them on the dashboard of her station wagon. They said, "WITHOUT LOVE I AM NOTHING!"

It meant nothing that supper was served on time, or that the laundry was all done, folded and put away, if her work was done with an attitude of drudgery. It meant nothing that she was able to juggle the schedules of her husband and children, as well as her own part-time job and hobbies, if she had no time left for a kind word, a loving touch, or even just a smile.

She realized that the single most important thing that she could ever do was to love her family. This was what the Lord wanted her to do. Those five words were so simple, yet so life-transforming. One day she told me, "Dr. Schuller, I began to live my life by love. I began to run my home on love power. It was as transforming as when I accepted Christ into my life. It brought happiness back into my life and into my home."

Without love, you are nothing. Whether you are a young mother, a doctor, a teacher, a psychologist, a businessman, a service man, a truck driver—whatever it is you do, whoever it is that you are—discover the simple truth that my friend, the young mother, discovered: *Without love I am nothing!*

Is love the right road? Is it really the greatest? Consider the answers to these questions:

Q: *What is society without love?*
A: *Society without love is a conglomerate of people who work, live, shop together—but never become a caring community.*

I remember a recent trip to Russia. While I was there, I could see how the Communist Party had tried to educate persons into being cold, calculating, intellectualized, rationalized creatures. It is like creating a person who basically becomes a computer responding to someone who pushes the button. Such a philosophy doesn't give humans enough credit. The Communist doctrines say that the human being, the emotional creature, is weak. It is at this point that Communism and Christianity are totally irreconcilable.

I subscribe to a couple of wire services and several years ago this story came over the wire service: "A religious fever is spreading across the Communist Soviet Union. In what is called 'an upsurge in religious practice in the Soviet Union,' tens of thousands of religious believers swarmed into the churches this past Easter. There they ate wafers, made crosses, and sang hymns to celebrate the resurrection of Jesus. Moscow's fifty-four churches, guarded by police and militant groups, were packed."

Why has such a phenomenon of social retrogression appeared in a so-called developed socialist country, in the land of the great Lenin? We know the answer: The normal, natural, healthy, whole human being is a creature whose emotional life has been allowed to blossom! Positive emotion is a mark of emotional health! By contrast, persons whose open, effervescent, ebullient, emotional instincts have been educated out of them or frozen out of them by society—such persons are not complete, healthy humans!

And what of the Nobel Prize-winning author Aleksandr Solzhenitsyn? Think of it—he was a product of Russia's educational systems, its indoctrination, its dialectical materialism. He had been protected from Western influences. Yet he has made this statement: "I myself see Christianity as the only living spiritual force capable of healing my land."

Incredible! Even after more than half a century, a totally repressive society based on total mind control has not been able to change the human being's deep heart hunger for love.

Q: *What is success without love?*
A: *Success without love is empty.*

Mary Nemec Doremus grew up in Palm Beach, Florida, where her family lived between the Kennedys and the Guccis, right on the ocean. She lived a privileged life, and by the time she was twenty had her own television show and was interviewing the "best" and most prominent Americans.

Then her father suggested that they go to Czechoslovakia to visit the land of their family's heritage. Her father's ancestors had been the gamekeepers and courtiers to the king there.

Shortly after they arrived in Czechoslovakia, however, the Russians invaded. Mary and her family heard shots being fired all night and day and witnessed children being blown apart.

One young boy they saw was proudly holding the Czech flag when he was shot. As the flag fell, another young boy picked it up.

Mary and the others were fortunate to get out of Czechoslovakia, and as they came across the border, after spending time lying on the floor with mattresses over their heads and tracer bullets ricocheting off the walls, these words came to Mary:

"Let the words of my mouth and the meditation of my heart
   be acceptable in Your sight, O LORD, my strength and my
   redeemer" (Ps. 19:14).

Mary Nemec's life was changed! Suddenly it didn't seem very important to see her name in lights. Suddenly it was very important to her to live! No longer was she interested in a movie career. She wanted to make her life count. She wanted to do something for her country and her God.

As soon as Mary stepped into the free world she was interviewed on the Huntley and Brinkley TV news program. Later, she gave over three hundred speeches around the United States. She encouraged young people to begin thinking about their country.

Ten years passed, during which time she met a young man named Ted Doremus, fell in love, and got married. She gave birth to two sons. Then Mary's parents urged her to join them on another trip. "Mary, China is just beginning to open up," they said. "We'd like to take you and the family to China to compensate for the traumatic visit to Czechoslovakia."

In China, Mary became ill with a virus. After she suffered from irritability, a low-grade fever, extreme weight loss, and intense pain all over her body for a year, doctors found a mysterious virus in her brain, her blood, her skin, and her cerebral spinal fluid. The result? Today, Mary relies heavily on the use of a wheelchair to conserve her energies and must take medication every twenty to thirty minutes during the day and several times at night for stabilization of her condition. Without it she becomes "limp," paralyzed and totally dysfunctional.

Her reaction? "Rather than groveling in my navel and demanding to know 'Why' from God, I've always tried to say, *'What do you want from me? Where am I supposed to be going?'* I knew there was a purpose that would be revealed to me at the right time. When I gave up the need to know, that was the healthiest thing that ever happened to me."

When I visited with Mary, I was so impressed with her beauty! She radiates genuine joy! She also told me, "I found that, from my bended knees in prayer comes the greatest standing I've ever done. I found that to be able to say that Jesus is my Lord and Savior is a very, very important thing for me to be able to say. This has been the basis for everything that I've done in life, including the National Challenge Committee on Disability. Through this organization, we're changing the way that America perceives individuals with disabilities. We're not childlike and dependent, but we're strong. And what we look or sound like has nothing to do with what we are able to do.

"When I sit here, the last thing I want you to notice about me is my disability. The first thing I want you to notice about me is my abilities. And I like to say that there's life *after* disability!"

Mary Doremus—what a wonderful example of someone who has discovered the beauty of living and living a life with love at the core. She has known what it is to be celebrated in society. She has known what it is to be a successful television personality. She has known what it is like to be superwealthy. And yet, as she discovered in Czechoslovakia, all of this is nothing without love. Even health was not as important as being able to give of herself to her country and to other disabled persons.

Q: *What is eloquence without love?*
A: *Eloquence without love is mere patter.*

In my chosen career as a minister, the ability to communicate ranks high among the gifts I sincerely desire. God only knows how often, how fervently, how passionately I have prayed, "Give me the gift of eloquence, Lord."

And God only knows how often He has answered that prayer. But I know this—He has answered it more often than I have deserved! And when I've experienced this exciting answer to prayer, it has been a "spiritual high!"

Why was the experience so fulfilling?

The answer I have found is that a beautiful feeling comes when a healing and comforting love is allowed to flow unobstructed through a human life.

I experience this same joyous emotion even more intensely and sincerely when I am alone as a pastor praying with a solitary soul in a private place.

What do these two different experiences have in common?

In both instances, whether the audience has been large—hundreds, thousands, even millions at a time—or whether it has been an audience of one, my happiness came from sharing a comforting, healing *love* with someone else!

Consequently, I am convinced that the happiness I am feeling at those times when the Lord grants me the gift of eloquence comes from the *love* I am feeling, not the oratorical experience. For the words, however colorful, however powerful, are nothing if they are not words that encourage, uplift, heal, and restore.

Q: *What is faith without love?*
A: *The most dangerous thing in the world!*

What is possibility thinking without love? If I have faith so that I can move mountains but do not have love, then you'd better watch out. Faith without love can be the most dangerous thing in the world! But faith, together with love, is a powerful, life-changing combination. The two go hand in hand. Faith and love are twins.

For years I believe I misunderstood a portion of 1 Corinthians 13. When I used to read the verse—"And now abide faith, hope, love, these three; but the greatest of these is love"—I thought Paul was in essence presenting three lovelies in a beauty contest. One was Faith, one was Hope, and one was Love. And when the judging was complete, Love won the crown, Hope was the first runner-up, Faith came in second. In other words, I had the mistaken impression that Faith, Hope, and Love were in competition with each other. That's not true; the three are a Holy Trinity, and love is what wraps them all together.

In a previous book, *The Be Happy Attitudes,* I put it this way:

> In the presence of Hope—
> faith is born.
> In the presence of Faith—
> love becomes a possibility!
> In the presence of Love—
> miracles happen!

Love: The Power Behind Faith!

Love is the power center behind a mountain-moving faith. When love is at the core of your faith, it puts five miracle-working powers into your belief.

1. Love Puts Renewing Power in Faith

When love is so strong it won't allow you to doubt for long, then it puts power at the center of your faith. Some people ask me, "Where do you get your faith?" My answer is simple: "I love Christ too much ever to doubt God!"

If love is at the core of your faith—for your work, for your project, for your dream, for your cause, for your husband, for your wife, for your children, for your friends—that faith will never quit. Where there is a passionate love, faith always comes back and renews the dream, tries again. Driven by authentic love, you will settle for nothing less than success. You will reorganize; reschedule; revise; reexamine; rededicate. But you will not *resign*! The kind of faith that never quits, the kind of faith that is constantly renewed, is faith that has love at the center.

2. Love Puts Realigning Power in Faith

When love is at the core of your faith, you constantly realign your faith to make sure that you are focusing on others, not *yourself*. And that's crucial.

I recently had to have my tires realigned. These were still new tires—only four months old and without many miles—but I could hardly drive down the freeway without the car almost jiggling apart. After my front wheels were realigned, though, the car no longer shook and was easy to control.

You and I must do this constantly with our faith. Realign your faith to make sure it's focused on service and not on self. Love at the power center will keep you smoothly on track.

3. Love Puts Restraining Power on Faith

Love keeps your faith from running over people just to get what you want. Remember, love without faith is impossible; and faith without love is unacceptable.

Once after I had finished one of my lectures at a sales conference, a businessman said to me, "I've got a problem. You know, I really believe I could expand my business to cover the whole country! But if I did it I would put a lot of little guys out of business. As a Christian I don't think I should do that, do you?"

"I don't think so either," I answered.

4. Love Puts Redeeming Power in Faith

When love is at the center of your faith, then your faith becomes a redeeming power. Instead of hurting people, you help people! Instead of being a destroyer, you become a builder! Instead of just being a teacher, for example, trying to draw your maximum salary and maximum benefits, you're primarily concerned about how you can mold and build complete persons out of those kids. And as a doctor you're not primarily concerned about how many fees you can attract, but how you can heal the whole person. And as a businessman you're not primarily concerned with profit margins, but how to serve people and their needs by delivering quality goods and services. And if you're a lawyer, you look upon yourself as a counselor helping people with distressing problems. And if you're a laborer or service technician, you really want to help people by doing great work honestly and at a fair price.

Faith is continuously *renewed*—when love is at the core.
Faith is continuously *realigned*—when love is at the core.

Faith is continuously *restrained*—when love is at the core.
Faith is continuously *redeemed*—when love is at the core.
Faith is continuously *rejoicing*—when love is at the core.

5. Love Puts Rejoicing Power in Faith

What good is faith if it leads to despair? With love—faith rejoices!

All of us have known of people who were positive and were terrific possibility thinkers. They made their goals, they achieved success, they were wealthy, they had power. And then, tragically, they ended up dead from an overdose. All the possibility thinking in the world is dangerous unless at the core there is love. It is love that gives the rejoicing power which keeps you energetic and joyful in your success! For after all, what is ultimate success but letting God's love and power flow through you! To summarize:

Faith *Stimulates Success!*
    I think I can!
    I think I'll try!
    I'm going to go for it!
Hope *Sustains Success!*
    I'm not going to give up!
    I'm going to be an H.I.T.—
    Hang-In-There person!
    Things will turn around!
Love *Sanctifies Success!*
    I'm going to share my success!
    I'm now able to help others!
    Now—I have something to give!

AM I GOING IN THE RIGHT DIRECTION?

Well, if you're going in circles, NO! You are not going in the right direction. Likewise, if you are standing still, the answer is NO!

If you insist on staying where you are, you'll waste the precious gift of love God has given you.

Oscar Hammerstein wrote in *The Sound of Music:*

> A bell is no bell til you ring it.
> A song is no song til you sing it,
> And love in your heart
> Wasn't put there to stay—
> Love isn't love
> Til you give it away."

Pass love on to someone who needs it. If we choose to be a reservoir of God's love, without allowing ourselves to be a channel of His love, we will soon see that love fails to generate joy power.

I recall standing at the bottom of Hoover Dam outside Las Vegas, Nevada. The guide was explaining the enormous turbines. "How much energy is being generated right now?" I asked. "Oh, nothing now," he answered. "The gates are closed; only when we allow the water to pour out of the reservoir through these turbines is energy generated!" Love's power comes as we allow love to pass through our lives to others.

Likewise, on my first trip to the Holy Land, the guide asked the question, "Do you know why the Sea of Galilee is alive with fish while the Dead Sea to the south of the Sea of Galilee is dead—salty, incapable of supporting any life? Remember, both lakes are filled with the very same water from the Jordan River." When no one offered an answer, he explained, "The Sea of Galilee gives all its water back! It takes the Jordan in from the north and gives it out as an extended Jordan River to the south. The Dead Sea takes in the water of the Jordan and holds onto all of it. It gives nothing back!"

Love Generates More Love! Love Generates Happiness!

Frank Laubach, a "world-class" missionary to the hungry, the illiterate, and the unlovely, once likened the human being to a common lawn sprinkler head. "It's worth about eighty cents," he said, "but attach the sprinkler head to a hose, let the water flow through, and it makes flowers grow. It makes the grass green. Suddenly you have parks, beauty, and food! Who can calculate the worth of that?"

Laubach continued, "God's plan for your life is to be a sprinkler head for Jesus Christ, letting His love flow through you, filling your world with happy love! Then every life becomes invaluable! The possibilities are endless! Then you can begin each day with a prayer I often pray: "Lord, show me the person you want to touch through my life today. Amen."

HERE, THEN, IS THE RIGHT WAY TO GO!

This is God's purpose for you, whoever you are, wherever you are. You can be a person through whom our Lord spreads His love and joy. Nothing else can compare with this satisfaction.

There are few people who have impressed me as much as my dear friends, Ole and Pat Nordberg. In fact, their story brings tears to my eyes every time I relate it. Their story summarizes the essence of this book, *Be Happy—You Are Loved!* It tells the *reality* of love, the *power* of love, and the *responsibility* to share love with others.

Pat was only thirty-two years old when the doctor faced her grimly in his office. Her husband Ole gripped her hand. The doctor looked at this bright young couple, the parents of a five-year-old boy. "Mrs. Nordberg," he said, "you have an aneurysm in the most inaccessible part of your brain. Your condition will get no better. You could die anytime. You might be lucky and live if nothing is done."

He paused and looked at their faces, which were numb with shock. Anticipating the inevitable question, he said, "Surgery? I'd say there's a ten percent survival possibility—that's all. I shall have to move the brain aside with my hands. If my finger slips or I don't handle it correctly, you could be paralyzed, blind, or a mental vegetable—if you live."

Pat and Ole could not speak. They were dazed as they somehow managed to walk out of the doctor's office. The drive home was silent, as speechless love flowed from heart to heart.

"Mommy, Mommy," their son cried as he ran into the waiting embrace of his beautiful mother. It was her son and husband that made the decision so difficult for Pat. Should she choose surgery with only a one in ten survival possibility? Should she let things go? Hope and pray that the next headache would never come? She remembered the first one some months before. She had felt the blood vessel break. She had felt the warm liquid flow around her brain under her skull before she lost consciousness.

New x-rays were taken. The diagnosis was the same as before. The aneurysm was still there.

"Why me? What have I done? I've been a good person." Self-pity mixed with anger as Pat wept alone in her bedroom.

"God is our refuge and strength, a very present help in trouble. Therefore, we will not fear, though the earth be removed, and though the mountains be carried into the midst of the sea; . . . God shall help her, . . . Be still, and know that I am God." These words came like sweet music into her mind. The verses from Psalm 46 brought with them a divine peace to the woman faced with a decision that no person should have to make. Now, with the power and strength of these words, she had her answer.

Pat called Ole. "Honey," she said, "I am no longer afraid. I know that if I die, God will provide someone better than I to love my son and my husband." She paused and with utter calmness said, "Ole, I am going to call the doctor and give him my decision—to operate."

Ole knew Pat's decision was the right one. Terribly concerned about the gravity of Pat's surgery, Ole immediately asked everyone he knew to pray for her. The neighbors joined in a circle of love. They spread the word of Pat's surgery from house to house on their street. "Ole is driving her to the hospital tomorrow. They don't give her much chance of ever coming back alive or with a normal mind, but she says this is the decision God led her to make."

The next morning a pall settled over the houses on the street. Children left for school, husbands went to work, but the women at home watched their clocks carefully. A neighbor called the other neighbors and said, "Let's all step out on our front steps and wave to Pat as she leaves and throw a prayer to her with a smile and kiss."

Quietly, coolly, and calmly, Pat entered the car as Ole carried her small overnight suitcase. He opened the garage door and backed out into the street. Pat saw them then, her neighbors all up and down the block, on both sides, waving and throwing her prayers with a smile and a kiss.

From house after house on both sides of the street, as Pat and Ole drove slowly away, neighbors waved goodbye, for the odds were that they would never see her again. Pat smiled. *She was loved.* It gave her strength and the peace to go through with an incredibly difficult, terribly dangerous, probably fatal surgery.

The surgeons cut Pat's skull open. Reaching into the cranial cavity, the doctor took the young mother's brain in his hands and ever so delicately removed the weak section of the major blood vessel that was threatening to blow. Delicately, gently, tenderly he returned the brain to its proper place, putting a protective plate over the hole in the skull. The entire skin of the scalp, peeled away for the surgery, was rolled back into place and stitched. Her hair would grow back in time—if she lived!

The surgeon, his task done to the best of his ability, went to face Ole. "Mr. Nordberg? It's all over for now. All we can do now is wait and pray. It may be days before we will know if Pat will live and what her condition will be."

Ole sat by Pat's bed. Her shaved head, wrapped in white bandages, still and unmoving in the center of the pillow, gave her a deathly appearance. Round the clock, hour after hour, day after day, nurses on duty waited, hoping for a sign of consciousness. Would her eyes open? Would her lips move? Would she be able to speak?

On the morning of the fourth day after surgery, the nurse on duty had turned her back for a moment when she heard a low but clear voice behind her. "Could you bring me some lipstick please, nurse?" Whirling, she looked at Pat, whose eyes were open and alert and, the nurse thought, who was mentally healthy enough to want to look pretty.

If only the sentences had kept coming so clearly. Over the next few weeks, Pat's wounded brain was unable to sustain normal speech. Words got mixed up and out of proper sequence. To compound the problem, her body was poorly coordinated. Would she ever be able to live a normal life?

Months passed. She was able to ride with her family to church again. "Pat," a church member stopped and asked her, "could you help out as a volunteer in the church school for our

Love without faith—
is impossible!
And
faith without love—
is unacceptable!

handicapped children's class? We need one adult for each child. Would you try, please?"

Pat didn't need to be asked twice! Here was a chance to prove that although her speech and body movements were unreliable, she could still be helpful. The events that occurred in that classroom changed her life. Soon after Pat volunteered she noticed an eight-year-old girl who was receiving little, if any, attention. When Pat asked about the girl, she was told, "Mary is only a vegetable. She has no potential for ever developing." Pat was deeply troubled. It was difficult for her to think that there were people who had no potential whatsoever.

One day, feeling empathy for Mary, Pat sat beside her on the floor, watching as Mary tore up pieces of paper and fluttered her mumbling lips with a finger. Then, when Mary looked at Pat, Pat smiled. Mary stared at Pat's smiling face, and then a miracle happened! The little girl crawled over and buried her head in Pat's lap and sobbed and sobbed.

Pat lovingly stroked Mary's head and back; she thought, *Dear Lord, if love alone will do this to a child, what would love plus an education do?*

She decided then and there to become a child psychologist. A long and impossible road lay ahead for Pat. Her first hurdle was to learn to drive a car so she could get to class. In order to develop the physical coordination to drive a car, Pat took Hawaiian dancing lessons. She passed her driver's test and enrolled in California State College in Fullerton.

Classes posed a new obstacle for Pat and her wounded mind. Remembering was a real problem for her. But she would not quit. She worked and worked and worked until she accumulated enough units to get her degrees. It took six long, tedious years, but she did it! Drawing from her aphasic experience, she wrote her master's thesis under the title, "Counseling Parents of Aphasic Children."

And along the way she learned tricks to help her with her

speech problem, until today her speech is perfect. People who meet Pat now are unaware of her past condition and have no idea what tremendous physical difficulties she has overcome.

Today, Pat, with her well-earned master of science degree, works with exceptional children in the public schools as a practicing school psychologist. She faced enormous challenges, yet she was happy. Why? Because she was loved! She was loved! Oh, was she loved! But she didn't just rest on that love. She gave it away as soon as she could, thereby multiplying her love as she shared it with children who were hurting.

"Be Happy—You Are Loved!" Does this statement describe you? Are you loved? Then give it away! When you do, you will find your life transformed from self-centeredness to other-centeredness. Attitudes will change from a greedy, "grab-all-I-can" attitude to a "What-do-you-need, How-can-I-help?" attitude.

In the assessment of any person—success or failure, saint or sinner, winner or loser, achiever or underachiever—the final judgment is not based on academic degrees nor honors nor medals nor talent nor training. No! The final exam is: Can you give and receive real love?

How do you become a "1-2-1-4-1" person? A "one-to-One-for-someone" person? A "God loves you . . . and so do I" person? For neither recognition nor fame nor wealth nor power can compensate for the lack of love coming into and flowing out of your life. No wonder St. Paul wrote, *"The greatest . . . is love."*

You are on the right road! Now get ready to turn onto the *free*-way!

THE ROAD OF LOVE:
BE BRAVE! TRAVEL THE *FREE*-WAY!

Real Love Liberates

"Love is patient."
    1 Corinthians 13:4

There is a strange paradox in love; a mysterious contradiction; a mystic ambiguity! To make love work we must release what we want to possess!

Some of my most delightful memories as a small child are the springtime days when baby chicks were delivered to our Iowa farm. I used to take the soft, fuzzy, newly-hatched little birds and rub what felt like silky fur against my cheek. Sometimes I would squeeze too tightly because I loved them so much and didn't want them to get away. "Don't hold so tight," my father warned.

"But I love the chick so," I protested.

"If you love it so much, you have to let it go," he said.

If you really love your wife, don't be so possessive; if you love your husband, don't be so jealous. Real love is not possessive. It does not manipulate or intimidate. *Real love liberates!* For it wants the object of its healthy love to blossom to its full potential!

It takes courage to love enough to let something or someone go. That's why this chapter title says, "Dare to take the *free-way.*"

Where I live in Southern California, freeways are an essential mode of transportation. This interconnecting web of lanes ties Southern California together from San Diego to San Francisco. These freeways, which are "free" of stop signs and traffic signals, allow motorists to whizz by on overpasses—and sail through cities.

149

The *free*-way road of love is a risky one. And its dangers and casualties frighten many from ever attempting it. Instead, they cautiously cling to the side roads, where their "love" is held in check by slower speed limits and *stop* signs!

I once sat in a class taught by the late psychotherapist, Erich Fromm. He pointed out that not all that passes for love is authentic or healthy! Some love is so possessive that it is the neurotic expression of an insecure person. Take the "possessive mother" or the "clinging vine" for instance! This possessive "love" arises from deep inner insecurities, low self-esteem, and fear.

Conversely, authentic and healthy love dares to take the *free*-way! A liberating love is reluctant to inhibit, prohibit, or solicit. Rather, it attempts to give the "green light" whenever possible. It encourages and patiently supports the person receiving the love.

I think that's what Paul meant when he said, "Love is patient." A patient love respects a person's need to take time and understands a person's need to grow. A patient love accepts the other person as he or she is, today! A patient love liberates in that it has faith that a person can change and can make it; it hopes that the one loved will someday respond to love; and, finally, it will work to help the one who is loved become what the person longs to be.

A LOVE THAT LIBERATES—IS A LOVE THAT *RESPECTS!*

Love respects—it respects the other person's need to take time to learn, time to grow, time to develop, time to improve.

Have you ever watched a young mother walk across a busy intersection, holding the hand of her little child, who hesitantly takes one wobbly step after another? You can sense the impatience in the drivers of the cars who are waiting to turn right. Patience is a virtue that many persons lose as soon as they get behind that mask of the windshield and are shielded from confronting people who will never be known or seen again.

On the other hand, with great patience, the mother appreciates her toddler's need to learn to walk, the child's need to grow gradually into an independent individual.

A LOVE THAT LIBERATES—IS A LOVE THAT *UNDERSTANDS!*

When you understand persons, you must respect their need to be themselves. It is encouraging that society has grown to the point where men and husbands are beginning to understand a woman's need to express herself through a career. I personally think it is a great thing to see women doing and accomplishing all that they can.

People are sometimes amazed when they look into the workings of the "Hour of Power," our television ministry. Several women hold prominent positions in our organization. And Arvella Schuller has been a partner with me in my ministry since we were married.

I met Arvella, who was the organist at the little Iowa church where I was a guest minister, when we needed to discuss the hymns and the music for the first service I would be conducting. Today, Arvella and I are still meeting to discuss each week's service. Arvella is program director for the "Hour of Power." She oversees a creative team of directors, musicians, and technicians who put together a worship service seen by over three million people every Sunday.

I understand and applaud Arvella's need for a career. Mixing a schedule as busy and complicated as ours requires a lot of give and take for both of us, but the rewards of such a partnership have been immeasurable—a thriving mutual love, admiration, and respect.

A liberating love understands, and when it understands, it is that much more prone to accept those who are loved and let them be who they are.

A LOVE THAT LIBERATES—IS A LOVE THAT *ACCEPTS!*

There are some things you cannot, will not *ever* change about your loved one, be he or she a child, a friend, a coworker, or a spouse. Can you accept that person as is—today? Even if the person stays that way for life?

A dear friend and employee of the "Hour of Power" is Shannon Wilkerson. Today, Shannon is vibrant and confident, which is a miracle considering that Shannon's early life was marred by physical and emotional abuse, mostly as a result of her mother's alcoholism.

In grade school, when most children went home to a smiling mom offering milk and cookies, Shannon went home to a mother who frequently was drunk and lying on the floor, unconscious. The few PTA meetings her mother attended were disrupted by her obnoxious behavior. Soon, parents of Shannon's schoolmates told their children not to play with the daughter of the drunken woman.

Believing that she was a freak, Shannon withdrew from friends and life in general. Her best friend became the television set in her bedroom, where she locked herself in at night to avoid her mother's verbal abuse.

Shannon's father was also a thorn in her life. Whenever he was home, Shannon avoided him because of his anger. Many times the young girl hid under the dresser in her bedroom to escape her fighting parents. At an early age Shannon learned that she couldn't trust anyone.

Then in junior high, and later in high school, Shannon started experimenting with drugs and alcohol. Shannon recalls, "I wanted so badly to be accepted by the other kids in my school. And smoking and taking speed helped me forget about the pain in my family."

Still addicted to TV, Shannon turned the set on one Sunday morning. "I awoke to a beautiful choir singing and a minister saying, 'Don't turn that channel. God loves you and so do I!' That caught my attention. I watched the 'Hour of Power' for the first time. I heard that Jesus loved me in spite of any wrong things I had done—even though I lived in a home full of turmoil."

Shannon's concept of God was transformed. No longer was God someone who punished people when they were bad and rewarded them with gifts when they were good. Instead, Jesus became real and personal—helping Shannon learn to accept herself. "Suddenly I knew," she says, "that I did not have to be a product of my parents and my home. I could be somebody special with God's help!"

With a new faith, Shannon withdrew from drugs and alcohol. She began to absorb herself in wholesome activities— the school band, Future Farmers of America, and gymkhana (barrel racing with her horse). Soon her efforts paid off. She earned the position of first-chair clarinet in the band, and working with animals helped her handle her resentments and fears.

"I knew I could be what God wanted me to be," Shannon says. "As I built up my self-esteem, I was able to prove to myself that I could make it. Every little success reassured me that I was right, made it easier to give up the drugs and my old negative patterns."

As she progressed through high school, Shannon continued to develop her young Christian faith. "The Lord showed me that I could trust Him," she recalls, "so I decided to ask Him for the biggest miracle in my life. I wanted my mother to be sober. I prayed and called New Hope, the telephone counseling ministry of the 'Hour of Power.' I wrote the ministry and they sent me literature on alcoholism, explaining that it was a disease, one for which I was not responsible. I read the literature in earnest and attended meetings for teen-agers of alcoholic parents. What I learned was that I was a co-alcoholic. A co-alcoholic is not someone who drinks, but someone who, by reactions, feeds the disease in the lives of the alcoholic in the family.

"As a child you want your parents to be there for you. But mine never were. I remember once when I was riding my horse and my dog ran out into the street and was hit by a car. I was so upset that I rode my horse to the front of our home. I wanted to cry in my mother's arms, but she had passed out on the floor.

"I learned to swallow my emotions. I grew up quickly. The bills were not always paid, so my brother and I had to take over that responsibility. The day the dealer came to repossess our cars, the two of us just sat on the fireplace and cried."

Convinced that she could get her mother to stop drinking, Shannon would search the house for empty bottles and wave them in front of her mother's face. Half-empty bottles of booze were dumped out and refilled with lemon juice, rubbing alcohol, or vinegar. But what Shannon thought would help her mother face her problem only aggravated her.

The problem came to a climax one rainy evening when Shannon took her mother's last bottle and dumped it down the drain. As Shannon talked on the phone to her best friend, her mother awoke from her drunkenness.

"She came up behind me and said in an angry voice, 'Shannon, I hate you and I'm going to kill you!' I turned and saw the knife in her hand. She was serious. I ran to my bedroom. Mother stumbled and fell as she chased me down the hall. Safely in my room, I stood in shock. Through the door I could hear her repeating how much she hated me. And then it happened—the knife came plunging through the door.

"I fell in a clump on the floor and cried. I was angry at God! I had read the literature. I had prayed. I had watched Dr. Schuller. I had done all I could do. What was wrong?"

Shannon's despair was suddenly interrupted by a quiet inner voice urging her to get up. She knew God was telling her to love the woman who had just tried to kill her! Pulling herself to her feet, Shannon opened the door to a very sick, very ugly woman, once more unconscious in the hallway. Shannon's emotions were in turmoil, her love struggling against her hate. "I am sorry it is like this," she found herself saying. "I love you very much and I am sorry."

At that moment a great burden lifted from her shoulders, and a sense of peace surrounded her. She knew her mother's disease would no longer control her life.

"Suddenly, I knew that everything was in God's hands. It was really 'letting go and letting God.' I had spent all my energies and time trying to fix her problem. Now, I began to invest my energies in myself. Instead of worrying about our arguments or trying to figure out how to make her sober, I decided to live my own life to the fullest. I refused to surrender to my mother's disease."

A year later Shannon's mom finally hit bottom—something that every alcoholic has to do before realizing he or she needs help. One morning this poor, sick mother decided she no longer wanted to wake up being sick! She called Alcoholics Anonymous, and together mother and daughter attended meetings to find physical and emotional healing. Shannon's initial doubts concerning her mother's sincerity were soon replaced with hope, and sixty days later Shannon's mother received special recognition for her sobriety. One year later a birthday cake celebrated the first anniversary of her freedom from the oppression of alcohol.

Eleven years have passed since Shannon's mother took her last drink. Three years ago, mother and daughter were baptized together in the Crystal Cathedral. Today, Shannon still finds the miracle hard to believe. "I never would have dreamed that such a total healing could take place," she says. "I always had faith that someday God would heal her, but the real miracle is the *forgiveness* that has taken place."

Shannon's mother is now remarried to another recovered alcoholic, and the two of them travel the country sharing their stories with hundreds of others still struggling to deal with their disease. "It is still difficult for me to listen to my mom speak," Shannon confesses, "because she always tells me how much she hated me—how I represented to her what she wanted to be. But then she always reaffirms her love for me."

A LOVE THAT LIBERATES—IS A LOVE THAT *BELIEVES!*

I first heard of W. Robert Gehring, M.D., through the letter he sent me in 1982. Now, he has published his story under the title, *RX for Addiction.*

He is a medical doctor. Surprisingly, his life was messed up, shot full of drug and alcohol addiction and demeaning sexual exploits. Then he tried to kill himself. He scrubbed up, pretending to be preparing for surgery, but instead he injected a drug in his veins, planning to end his misery for good.

However, he regained consciousness. Standing at his side was one of the hospital's prominent staff physicians. Dr. Gehring had no doubt that he would be evicted from his position at the hospital.

Imagine his shock when the doctor said to him, "Bob, I have no intention of having you dismissed from the hospital. I've come to try to save you. All I want is for you to come to church with me."

Robert Gehring had tried everything else. He decided to try church as well. To his amazement he found what he had been looking for. He encountered Jesus Christ and was saved—all because a fellow doctor, a Christian man who believed in God and believed in Dr. Gehring, gave him the gift of love and helped him receive the gift of faith.

Have faith in others. They may still be just seeds waiting to sprout. But the potential is there, just under the surface. If a relationship is nurtured with the warmth of love, if it is watered with positive thoughts and affirmations, if the negatives can be tenderly weeded out or choked out by the new positive feelings of self-esteem that will appear as a result of your love, you will be amazed at what will bloom in the most unlikely spot!

If this seems impossible to do, then let me share a prayer that might help:

> *FAITH*
>
> Lord, I believe
> In the sun, even when
>   it is behind the clouds;
> In the seed, even when
>   it lies unsprouted under the ground;
> In faith, even when I have been betrayed;
> In love, even when I have been rejected;
> In hope, even when I have been hurt;
> In God, even when
>   You do not answer my prayers.
> Amen.

A LOVE THAT LIBERATES—IS A LOVE THAT *HOPES!*

You can be patient with others if you have *hope* that eventually they will respond to your love. If someone you love is reticent to accept your love, then ask yourself, "Could they be holding back from love because they are hurt, crushed, broken?"

In my office I have a beautiful photograph of Freedom on my wall. Freedom is the famous American bald eagle.

On December 30, 1980, an Iowa farmer walking through his field saw a large wounded bird flapping his wings awkwardly in the snow. The bird tried desperately but couldn't fly. The farmer approached the bird and was shocked to see that it was a bald eagle with a wing badly shattered by some hunter's poorly aimed buckshot. The proud bird, a national treasure that is protected by law, had been left floundering. The bird was four to five years of age and stood two feet high. His wings, even though one was broken, measured six feet from point to point.

The Iowa farmer had heard about the Raptor Rehabilitation Center for birds of prey, connected with the University of Minnesota. So on December 31, 1980, the bird was brought to Raptor. The wounded wing gradually healed, and Dr. Reptick, the founder of the Raptor Center, said that he thought the bird might fly again.

On February 8, 1981, three months later, the bird was sent by airplane to Washington, D.C., where he appeared at Constitution Hall as part of the welcome home to the hostages held in Iran. And later in a special program, a tribute to the men missing in action in Vietnam, he became a famous eagle. He was brought back from Washington to Preston, Wisconsin, where four hundred people looked on as the director of the Raptor Clinic said, "I think we can trust him to live in the wilds again."

The leather thongs were snipped at each foot, and the bird stretched his wings slowly, cumbersomely. He flapped them, flying very low to the ground, and then began to soar over the river and the hills. A photographer snapped the picture, and a famous painter painted the scene and sent me a print. It's entitled simply *Freedom*.

Once this proud bird was healed of his hurts and his wounds, he was able to fly again. Perhaps there is someone you know and love who is hurting and carries deep scars, wounds that keep him from responding. Be patient. There is hope. Believe that healing will come with time and unceasing love!

A LOVE THAT LIBERATES—IS A LOVE THAT *WORKS!*

It's not enough just to respect, to accept, to understand, to believe in, and to hope for those you love. You also need to *work* at loving them.

We have a specialized outreach at the Crystal Cathedral to prisoners. Many of our people work year round conveying love to the men and women inmates of Chino. The parishioners' love is patient and kind. They go to the prison every week. They write to the inmates and send them literature. But most of all they bake cookies!

Every Christmas, the Crystal Cathedral congregation gets together to bake fourteen thousand dozen cookies. That's a lot of cookies! They are all handmade—chocolate chip, oatmeal-raisin, peanut butter, sugar, you name it—and they are baked in the kitchens of our people's homes.

Then they are lovingly wrapped and boxed in care packages that include one of the gifts that we give out on Sundays to our television congregation. Some boxes have rainbow suncatchers in them that say, "When it rains, look for the rainbow." Others have crosses. Each Christmas gift box also includes literature, along with stationery with stamped envelopes! Each box is carefully wrapped and individually handed to an inmate by one of our volunteers who shakes hands, looks the person in the eye, and says, "Merry Christmas! God loves you and so do I!"

I have long believed in the beauty and the power of this

simple sentence, but recently I was absolutely shocked to face
in an unlikely spot the results of this statement of love and of
the prison ministry.

My son, Bob, and I were on our way to lunch when I noticed
that my gas tank was nearly empty. Bob said, "Do you have
money?"

"No, but I have some credit cards," I answered. With that
assurance we pulled into a Texaco station, the first station we
came to.

"Fill it up," my son said to the young man who came to serve
us. He filled it up. I gave him the credit card.

He looked at it and said, "Sir, this card's no good. It expired
three months ago. Do you have any cash?"

I was in a predicament. Bob didn't have enough cash either. I
said, "I don't have any cash on me. But look, don't you
recognize me?"

"I never saw you before in my life," he said.

"I'll give you a clue. My name is Schuller."

"Never heard of it."

I was at a loss. I finally said, "I don't have anything else to
give you. You may keep the credit card. I'm sure Texaco will
honor it. My credit is impeccable. And if they won't accept this
credit card, you can check me out in the telephone book . . . .
You can call me . . . . I'll pay you cash! Plus interest for the
trouble!"

He agreed.

Later, while Bob and I were having lunch, I happened to find
my *new* Texaco card! I said to my son, "It's a long way back to
that gas station, but I think we ought to go."

When we pulled into the station the attendant came
running. "Oh, I'm glad to see you!" he said. "I told my boss
about it and, boy, did I get it! He told me, 'Everything is on
computer today. As soon as that outdated credit card hits the
computer, it's going to come back here and you are going to
have to pay that bill out of your own salary.'"

The choice
to believe
and love
is a God-given
option
that's always
open
to every person!

P.S. Now then—isn't God
good?!

The agitated young man continued, "You know, I haven't had this job too long. I really want to do good at it. So I really am glad to see you! When my boss looked at the card, he recognized your name. He helped me realize that you are Dr. Robert Schuller. I didn't put it together at first! I just got out of jail. It was while I was in prison that I read the books that were written by a Dr. Robert Schuller. I've got to tell you, you changed my life!"

"Jail?" I said. "Was it Chino?"

"Yes."

"Did you get a box of cookies and gifts?"

"You bet. And, Dr. Schuller, last year in the gift box there was a little wooden cross. That was the only gift I had to send to my little son. I read the three books, and I came to realize that I was in jail because I had a bad attitude."

After I handed him my new credit card I reached in my briefcase, got out a copy of *The Be Happy Attitudes*, autographed it, and gave it to him.

A life liberated! A man saved—because these were "God loves you . . . and so do I" people, "one-to-One-for-one" persons, who loved enough to work at putting someone on the *free*-way to happiness.

THE ROAD OF LOVE:
CATCH IT! THE
EXPRESS-WAY!

Real Love Communicates

"Love . . . is kind; love is not jealous or boastful."
  1 Corinthians 13:4

I f you ever have found the road of loving relationships to be rutted, narrow, and littered with rocks, you probably need to change roads—to find the *express*-way. You may need to learn how to express love more effectively. I have seen, after years of marital and other counseling, that rocky relationships frequently are a result of misunderstandings bred by inadequate communication.

I heard the other day of a young woman who went to see her lawyer about getting a divorce from her husband. At the first meeting the lawyer said, "Well do you have any grounds for this divorce?"

"Yes, an acre-and-a-half," she answered.

"No," he said, "what I mean is, do you have a grudge?"

"We don't have a garage, but we have a carport."

The lawyer was getting very frustrated with this first meeting. Taking a wild stab he said, "Well, does he beat you up?"

"Oh no! I get up before he does every morning!"

At this point the lawyer threw up his hands and said, "Well, then what's the problem?"

"I don't know," she said, thoughtfully. "We just can't seem to communicate."

Communication is the key to making your relationships with others work. Without it, the doors will remain locked. Feelings will be suppressed. Misunderstandings will abound. Expressing love is an art that I'd like to help you master, but it will take some effort—and some time.

FIND TIME TO EXPRESS LOVE

Make time to find the *express*-way. Take the time to express love. Schedule "express times" into your calendar.

My wife, Arvella, and I have a date night every week. Mondays are our date nights, and *nobody* interferes. My secretary has orders that absolutely *nothing* can be scheduled on Monday night. My children know it is futile to try to reach my wife or me on Monday night.

This date night is our express-love night. It is the time of the week when we go someplace alone and get to know each other again. In just one week's time, so much can happen, so many misunderstandings can occur that it's vital for us to sit down and lovingly discuss what we've been feeling the last week and what we are expecting in the upcoming week.

In my opinion, this weekly date night has been one of the secrets of my successful marriage of over thirty-five years to my first and only wife!

This is not easy—our schedules are FULL. We are both extremely busy. We are constantly pulled on by our children, associates, friends, social and business obligations, and opportunities in ministry. A marriage can only take pulling for six days. On the seventh, we need a respite—a chance to be together as husband and wife, friend and companion, free from the tensions and distractions of everyday life.

Interestingly, Dr. Joyce Brothers once suggested a similar technique in parent-child relationships. When asked how parents could ease sibling rivalry, Dr. Brothers answered, "Give each child a special night of the week when they get to stay up one-half hour later than their brothers or sisters. Use that time to talk and listen to and love that child. You'll be amazed at how much that weekly time will do for you and your children."

Communicating love takes time, and expressing love requires a certain amount of know-how. In my many years as a pastor, television preacher, author, and lecturer, I have learned something about communication, and when it comes to relationships, there are three sides to expressing love: See It, Say It, and Show It.

SEE IT!

"All I want is a look!"

We all cry out at one time or another for wordless, matchless communication. We all long to feel the love that can be expressed tenderly and sincerely with a look of love.

This simple, but heart-enriching form of communication is one of the first to be neglected. We find ourselves buried in a television show, needlework, dishes, weeds to pull, bank sheets to balance. We fail to take the moment, the few *seconds* to look up from our work or activities and look into the hearts of those we love.

It is essential that we learn to recapture this art of speaking with the eyes, for love can look deep into the hearts and read the unspoken distress signals. Frequently, the words that reveal the deepest reaches of our soul are too painful to say out loud. But the eyes will tell the truth. When the lips deny, the eyes can frequently see what's really going on within.

The eyes can see the truth, and they also can see if the message is getting across. They let us know if the listener is really listening and comprehending.

When we communicate within our family we make it a point to look each other in the eye. We do not throw out information in passing when the other person is working, reading, or watching TV. We make sure others take a break and stop and listen with their eyes.

Arvella and I were especially concerned with this when our children were small and we were disciplining them. When I used to reprimand one of the kids or was talking to them of love, I often said, "Look at me!" Direct eye contact established the fact that I meant what I said. It insured that my child really was listening and that I had been heard.

So! Let us not fail to understand the ability of the eyes to speak of love—whether it be a loving look of discipline and correction, or a look of loving approval.

I shall long remember my father's amazing ability to speak with his eyes. He was a reserved person, and although he usually sat quietly in any large room filled with his married sons and daughter and grandchildren of all ages, without his saying a word, we all knew how very much he loved us. He was truly a man of few words, but his eyes and face assured us of his love.

A quotation from a woman who had fifty happy years of marriage says it perfectly: "Early in our marriage, we learned to see through each other . . . and still enjoy the view!" (*Reader's Digest*, 1977).

SAY IT!

Words are the obvious building materials of communication. Once we have *seen* it, it's important to *say* it, for verbalizing our feelings does two things: First, it confirms to the other person that what they believe they are feeling is indeed true. Secondly, just saying "I love you" to someone does require a certain amount of basic commitment from you.

Saying that we care, whether it be words of praise or words of correction, is one of the more difficult and challenging parts of communication. Since verbal communication is such an essential stone in the foundation of a loving relationship, volumes have been written on this subject by psychologists and psychiatrists. However, nothing I have read on the fine art of communication has been as practical and as helpful as what I learned from the late Dr. Henry Poppen.

Dr. Poppen was a wonderful friend and served as the first minister to the Keenagers (senior citizens group) in our church. He had been a missionary to China and was imprisoned when the Communists took over the Chinese government. Earlier Dr. Poppen had used his communication gifts to skillfully negotiate with the Japanese captors, persuading them to feed hundreds of thousands of starving Chinese villagers.

One day I asked Henry, "What is the secret to your success in communicating with others?"

His answer was power-packed. "Four words," he answered. "Be *friendly*. Be *fair*. Be *frank*. Be *firm*."

I have followed his advice as a husband, a father, and a pastor, and I have to tell you—it works!

1. Be friendly. "Love . . . is kind."

The power of words! They can hurt; they can maim; they can destroy a relationship. On the other side of the coin, words can enrich, save, and heal.

I once knew a girl who had unsuccessfully tried various methods of suicide. Her life was salvaged by three small words. A man whose friendship was very important to her said to her therapist, "I will do anything I can to help her. *She's worth it!*"

Those three words, "She's worth it!" totally transformed this girl's life. She began to see her worth for the first time. She no longer wanted to die. She was valued. She had something to offer to others—herself! She wanted to live.

If only we could all be so thoughtful and generous with our words, and restrained from making negative comments, even in jest. I am amazed at the number of people who callously throw out negative comments about others under the guise of humor. In our family I have long had the rule that we are not to partake in negative humor. We do not call each other names, such as "fatso," or "turkey," or "jolly green giant." For even though everybody may laugh at the time, the other person most assuredly ends up later in the privacy of his room, wondering if there isn't some truth in the jest. After all, if there wasn't some truth in it, then why would everybody laugh!

Be friendly when you communicate. Be kind. Choose your words carefully. If you are dissatisfied with your relationships, I suggest that you take an inventory of your conversations. Are they positive? Are they kind? Do they build others up?

It's interesting in studying 1 Corinthians 13 to note that Paul says "Love . . . is kind," and then almost in the same breath, "Love is not jealous or boastful." Ogden Nash once wrote:

> To keep your marriage brimming,
> With love in the loving cup,
> Whenever you're wrong, admit it!
> Whenever you're right, shut up!*

In other words, "Don't boast!"

I think it's important to mention at this point that at times silence, refraining from speaking, can be the most friendly form of communication.

It's easy to boast and overlook the fact that good news for you may be bad news for someone else. And it takes a great deal of sensitive respect for another's feelings to decipher which is which. Think of it:

- Your promotion, when your friend and colleague has been passed up, may well be good news for you but may be bad news for your friend who is still waiting.

---

*I Wouldn't Have Missed It (Boston: Little Brown, 1962). Used by permission.

- The news of your marriage engagement is good news for you, but it may be bad news for your single friend. Your diamond ring may only remind her of her lack.
- Your pregnancy is good news for you. But it may feel like bad news for your friend who has been trying to have a baby and has been unable to conceive.

It is a rare friend who is able to handle a friend's good news when he is not as fortunate. So before you are quick to share your "good" news, stop and think, "Will this hurt this person or help them? Will it inspire and encourage, or will it discourage and depress?"

If you're not sure what the answer would be—then I would suggest that you keep your good news to yourself!

2. Be fair. Love doesn't make unreasonable demands.

Love does not insist on its own way. That is being fair! How do you know what's fair and what's not? My advice (it has worked for me) is be honest and ask, "Do you think I'm being fair? What do *you think* I should do to help you?" Then remember the old American Indian proverb, "Never ask one to walk with you till you have walked one day in his moccasins."

3. Be frank.

"How can I be frank and friendly at the same time?" you ask. "There are times when I need to tell those I love that they are having problems. After all, you don't let your wife go out of the house with a tear in the back of her dress, do you? And I can't let my loved ones say things or do things that will ultimately hurt them."

An age-old conflict! A timeless question! Is it possible simultaneously to maintain a sense of loyalty to another's feelings and loyalty to one's own integrity?

If we read further in 1 Corinthians 13, we find a clue. St. Paul writes, "If you love someone, you will be loyal to him [or her] no matter what the cost" (TLB).

Loyalty is the key word. Loyalty, by its nature, implies honesty. If you look at any large corporation, you'll see what I mean. A chief executive may have many people working for him. Of these some are true-blue, loyal employees. They are the ones who love the company and the president enough to be honest with him. But there are also the "yes-men" and "yes-women" who care only about their own careers, and consequently, they tell the president only those things that will further their own advancement in the company.

Loyalty and honesty are essential to any love relationship. *Constructive* honesty, rooted in love, can often open the lines of communication in *any* relationship.

I have emphasized the word *constructive* and thereby have chosen to qualify the term *honesty*. I believe that various degrees of honesty do exist, ranging from the constructive to the destructive. We may "speak the truth" and hurt people in the process. Not all honesty is valuable, and not all words of truth are rooted in love.

Constructive honesty builds up, but destructive honesty tears down. Constructive honesty looks for solutions, while destructive honesty points out the weak spots. Destructive honesty hurts. Constructive honesty heals.

Consider the wise words of my daughter-in-law, Donna, who has the challenging task of being a pastor's wife. That kind of position requires the very special gift of being constructively honest. It is a gift I see in my wife, Arvella, and recently I saw Donna exhibit the same ability.

We were all gathered at the family home after a Sunday of morning worship services. Our son Bob had delivered the message for the "Hour of Power," which he does from time to time. We were all relaxing over a delicious dinner that Arvella had made. In the midst of the laughter, Bob turned to Donna and said, "Well, how did I do this morning?"

"Very well! I was really proud of you, Bob!" Donna said.

"Yeah? How did you like the story about . . . ?" He mentioned one of his illustrations.

Donna paused. The story had not gone over that well. Should she be honest and tell Bob that he shouldn't repeat the story—maybe ruining the family gathering, not to mention Bob's day? Or should she lie and tell him how wonderful it was only to hear him repeat it in the future?

I shall never forget her wise answer, "Bob. The story was O.K. But, you know, you have others that I like a lot more!"

Bob's deep baritone voice rolled with laughter. "Don't I have a wonderful wife? Did you notice how beautifully she put that?"

He put his arm around Donna and said, "O.K., honey, I get the picture. Thanks."

Honesty and integrity are rooted in loyalty. The truly honest person remains loyal to the other person's feelings and is aware that it is possible to be honest, frank, and positive at the same time. Recognize this: You don't have to reflect things the way they are *now* to be totally honest. You can reflect things as they have been—reminding a person of when he was exceptional, as Donna did. Or you can project the possibilities and the opportunities of what someone can do and become without losing integrity. We can reflect in love what the person *can be*.

Consider these examples:

- "You can be a really great student!"
  —A father to his child who is struggling in school.
- "You would be a knockout if you lost a few pounds."
  —A mother to an overweight child.

Real love sees people not as they are, not as they were, but as they can become. This is love at its best. This is the love Jesus has for us. He sees us not as we are, but as we can become. This love is healing and constructive.

If you love someone, you will be loyal no matter what the cost. Jesus paid the cost of His loyalty to us: death on the cross. He only asks in return that we love others as best as we can and that we reflect Christ's love as clearly and beautifully as possible.

4. Be firm.

We have all heard the term *tough love.* Parents, chief executive officers, persons in the final seat of authority know that to vacillate is to send signals of weakness into negotiations, and love is a process of negotiation! "Love . . . is kind; love is not jealous or boastful; it is not arrogant or rude" but love does not mean that we let people run over us and give them exactly what they want. It does not mean that we tell people what they want to hear, even though the truth may upset them.

Indeed, there are principles which you must never compromise. There are moral values that must never be sacrificed. Do you remember Tevye, the father in *Fiddler on the Roof?* He is a tremendous example of compromise. When each of his daughters asks for his permission or blessing to marry the man of her choice, he discusses the difficult matter with himself. He argues both sides of the issue. "On the one hand. . . ," he says, and then he adds, "But on the other hand. . . ."

Often his decision involves compromising his ideas of proper *social* structure. But with his last daughter he reaches the point when he says, "There is no other hand!" When it calls for him to compromise in his *religious* beliefs, he cannot do it. This is a line that he cannot cross.

There is always a point beyond which you *cannot* compromise!

EXPRESS LOVE: SEE IT! SAY IT!
NOW SHOW IT!

The gift of touch is a wonderful and unique way to communicate love. It has been shown that children need touch so much that in extreme cases a child may die without it! They need to be cuddled, even as newborns. Perhaps that's why some of the prominent hospitals in Southern California now have baby cuddlers on their neonatal staff. These men and women go to the hospitals and do one thing—they cuddle the newborn babies. While mothers are resting and recuperating and while the nurses are busy tending to the babies' medical needs, the baby cuddlers hold the babies, they stroke them, they talk to them, and they love them.

One baby cuddler was featured recently on television news. She was shown holding a little premature baby, with his stocking cap on his head to keep in his body warmth. His wrinkled little face was cradled in the cuddler's arms. The lovely, white-haired grandmother rocked this baby and talked to him. Suddenly the infant gave a funny, crooked little smile.

"See?" the baby cuddler exclaimed. "He's smiling. He's happy. That's because he's loved!"

Not only the babies benefit from this program; the baby cuddlers say that they do it as much for themselves as for the infants. There are many such programs across this great country. With all the hurting people in the world, there is no excuse for anybody not to take an opportunity to show love to others.

We all need to look creatively for ways to say "I love you" through the things we do. Actions *do* speak loudly.

Dr. Howard House and his brother Dr. William House are the founders and directors of the House Ear Institute, a leading institution for research to help the hearing-impaired. The

House brothers developed the cochlear ear implant, which has enabled children with supposed permanent hearing loss to hear sounds—many for the first time in their lives. Recently at a wedding reception, Howard presented one of his favorite poems, a stanza by Odell McConnell:

> Love is a verb as well as a noun;
> Love means a smile and never a frown.
> To love is to do and not just to feel,
> For unless you express it, love isn't real.

Love in action. That is a love that really communicates. Let me suggest a definition of love in action:

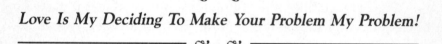

Love Is My Deciding To Make Your Problem My Problem!

With this definition of love, you don't have to be a minister, a counselor, a psychiatrist, or a doctor to know what I'm talking about. Whatever your profession or career, you can express love for others in whatever you do.

Take Kenneth Hahn, for example. Kenny, who is the supervisor of Los Angeles County, has used his position in politics to live love and express love by creating programs that help people with their problems. You may not realize it, but as a result of his decision to make others' problems his problem, Kenny has saved countless lives—perhaps even yours! No matter what city, what county, what state you live in, if you have been helped by the paramedics of your community, you can thank Kenny Hahn.

The paramedic program in America started in Los Angeles in 1970, because when one man, a wonderful Christian, heard about the problem, he wouldn't let anything stop his solving it.

Dr. Walter Graf, who was Chief of Cardiology at Daniel Freeman Memorial Hospital in Los Angeles, once said to Kenny, "You are good at solving problems. How would you like to endorse a plan where you can save a life a day?"

Kenny responded, "Me? How can a politician save a life a day?"

"I think the county firemen can be trained to render emergency aid, the same as is given by a doctor or a nurse, for the first hour in the field," Dr. Graf replied.

Kenny couldn't see why his help was needed. He asked, "Why doesn't the medical profession do it?"

"Well," Dr. Graf said, "we have to change the whole state law in order to have firemen trained to be paramedics, because they need to apply morphine in the first hour of treatment for a heart attack. And the Health and Welfare Code of the State of California states that only a doctor or a registered nurse can prescribe morphine."

So Kenny Hahn had to try first to change state law. He was told it would be impossible, but Kenny would not take "No" for an answer. He worked through red tape to gain support of his new bill allowing trained firemen to prescribe morphine in emergency situations. Finally, the bill passed through the California Assembly and the Senate, but it was opposed by the California Medical Association, as well as by the American Medical Association. The State Firechiefs Association was opposed also. They didn't want the firemen to practice medicine.

Then the supervisor got a call from Governor Ronald Reagan. "Kenny, I'm going to veto that bill you're interested in," he said.

"Governor, before you make your final decision," Kenny pleaded, "let me come up to Sacramento and explain to you how it works."

He went to Sacramento and talked to the governor. He explained, "The county fire department will cross all lines of the eighty-four cities in Los Angeles County. They will be able to reach eight million people. The county fire department will get the call. They will have a base hospital that will be able to monitor the person's heart attack right at the scene."

The governor looked at Kenny and said, "Did you say that they will cross all city lines?"

"Yes."

Governor Reagan signed the bill, even though so many opposed it. He said to Kenny later, "My own father died when city police ambulances wouldn't cross jurisdictional lines."

Imagine Mr. Hahn's joy then, at a paramedics reception after the first year, when twelve people who had been pronounced dead but were saved by trained paramedics came up to him and said, "Thank you." In 1985, in Los Angeles County alone, the paramedics responded to 101,000 calls for help.

Kenny is also responsible for a freeway telephone system that has helped countless stranded motorists in Los Angeles County. Again, Kenny was inspired by a need, and he responded with love and concern.

One day he was on the Harbor Freeway when he saw a woman climbing over the bank. Kenny pulled over and learned the woman had run out of gas and was stranded and lost on this busy, dangerous freeway. Kenny took her to a gas station, got her some gas, came back, and filled up her tank.

That experience convinced him that Los Angeles County needed emergency phones along the freeway system—one every mile. Now there are three thousand telephones on every freeway in the county. This is the only county in the United States that has emergency telephones. And already over five million motorists have used them.

Kenny Hahn—I am proud to call him a friend, because he shows his love by deciding to make others' problems his problem. He doesn't just talk about it. He does it—to the very best of his ability!

*Love
is
my decision
to make
your
problem—
my
problem!*

THE *EXPRESS*-WAY EXPRESSES LOVE—BY DOING SOMETHING TO HELP!

Ralph Showers is another example of someone who makes others' problems his own. As a disabled farmer he is in the business of communicating the meaning of love to hundreds of mentally retarded young people and young adults. His organization, called Rainbow Acres, consists of three ranches, where ninety mentally retarded people are cared for by a staff of fifty, with many of the mentally retarded working to help pay their own way. Rainbow Acres has helped nine other ranches start across the United States, as well as one in Japan. The ranch does not take any government support and is becoming self-sufficient.

The man who built this tremendous organization was told when he was in the seventh grade that his IQ was 84—"dull-normal." The "experts" suggested that he not continue school, but his family reminded him that God had created him and had breathed life into him. If God believed in him, so did they.

Ralph did have a tough time getting through school. Yet he managed to get his undergraduate degree and then his theological education. He served as a pastor after he got out of seminary and was ordained in the American Baptist Church. He served churches in Hawaii, Arizona, and California. Then he had an intuition, a compulsion to acquire ten acres of land in Arizona.

He had no idea what he was supposed to do with the land other than to build a ranch on it. After he took the step of faith to purchase the land, the Lord gave him the dream of a ranch for the mentally retarded. Ralph began to work diligently on the dream. Then, in 1973, while Ralph stood atop a barn that was being moved to the ranch, he backed into a power line bearing 7,200 volts of electricity. His hands and arms were burned so badly that gangrene set in and both hands had to be amputated.

Today, Ralph has two hooks for hands. But he says that his handicap has actually been a blessing, because he now is able to work that much better with handicapped people and share with them and love them; he knows exactly what it means to be handicapped.

Ralph loves people who frequently have been forgotten by others. He sees their possibilities, what they can contribute to society. Approximately three out of every hundred people in America are mentally or physically handicapped. But Ralph believes that every person is created for a purpose, for a reason. And he has shown that it doesn't matter whether or not legs are lame, eyes are sightless, ears cannot hear, minds are slow, or hooks have replaced hands. Whatever the handicap might be, God has a purpose for each life!

I asked Ralph one day, "People with severe handicaps, are they happy?"

Ralph replied, "Oh, of course we have all the normal problems, the ups and the downs like everybody else, but I wouldn't exchange living with this group of people for anything on the face of the earth. There is simplicity; there's no question about it. But their faith, their excitement, everything about them is special, and it's a wonderful experience to love them and be loved by them."

It's possible for *all* of us to be a success at communicating love—*if* we will take the time to use the *express*-way! Yes, it means we become "God loves you . . . and so do I" people, "one-to-One-for-someone" persons!

Now, we'll *express* love! We'll see it! Say it! And show it!

THE ROAD OF LOVE:
PAY THE PRICE!
USE THE
TOLL-WAY!

1

Real Love Compromises

"Love does not insist on its own way."
    1 Corinthians 13:5

Two boys were trying to play on a hobby horse outside a department store. It was one of those horses where you put a quarter in a slot and the horse goes up and down. They were both trying to ride at the same time when one boy said, "You know, if both of us didn't try to get on at the same time, I could have a much better ride."

There's a lot of truth to that statement! And we adult drivers on the road of life could take a lesson from those boys. Too often we vie for the same spot on the road, each trying to pass the other. Our pride can't handle being in second place, yet not everyone can come in first.

This "push and shove" way of life will only lead to frustration and is quite dangerous. And unless we are prepared to take the *toll*-way, are willing to wait in turn at the gates, pay our dues, and graciously drive side-by-side with fellow travelers, we may find we're not even on the road of love.

We've reached a point in our world where unless we compromise, we're all going to be bruised over the same hobby horse, and nobody is going to have a decent ride. Many of us never learned to give and take, even after we grew up. We are guilty of thinking that we have earned a right to demand our own way—in marriage, in business, in parenting, in every life relationship. Many of us are guilty of acting like children, of stating through our actions, "I want what I want, when I want it!"

But Paul, in his love letter to us, gives us a clue on how to secure lasting, happy relationships. He encourages us to give when we feel like taking. He encourages us to take the nobler route—the way of compromise. Although compromising appears to be the weaker stance I contend that it is really the stronger. Compromise requires a love forged from steel. It requires a deep, mature love to take the long view—to see beyond the momentary "high" of winning an argument and thereby winning the relationship.

This is a difficult concept for most of us to grasp, for we have been warned from childhood never to compromise. So-called "principles of success" often suggest that we must hold unwaveringly to our beliefs and our plans. We are taught that the laurels go to the strong. The victories go to the brave. The accolades go to the resolute. So we feel that we should fight for our rights. We should never back down.

Right? Sometimes. But not always!

I am a strong advocate of firm convictions, of being true to commitments, of climbing the mountain, of tunneling through the difficulties, but there are times when we must learn to compromise. Sometimes it is in our best interests, as well as others', to give a concession to our "opponents."

Where could we find an example of compromising love at work? Well, one place to look is in the Lennon home. As you know, the Lennon sisters, who sang on the Lawrence Welk television show, all come from the same family. The sisters who form the singing group are the four oldest of a family of eleven children. Yes, eleven! Mrs. Lennon is the mother of five boys and six girls.

Now, I've got to tell you, there's no way that a family of that size can live harmoniously, and there is no way that four sisters can sing so harmoniously unless there is a tremendous capacity to compromise.

The sisters say in their book, *Same Song, Separate Voices*, *

---

*Round Table Publishing, 933 Pico Blvd., Santa Monica, CA 90405.

that they sang from the time they were very little. They learned their harmonies from their father and his brothers who used to sing and rehearse at their house. At first the sisters sang mostly for church functions.

But one of the girls, Dee Dee, went to school with Lawrence Welk, Jr. He heard the girls sing one night and said, "Gosh, my dad has a TV show and he's looking for talent. I'm going to tell him about you."

A few weeks later young Lawrence called and said, "My dad's home in bed. He's sick with a cold and he can't get out. So come sing for him."

They did. That was around Christmas of 1955, and Mr. Welk had the girls sing on his Christmas Eve television show. The Lennons were on the show every Saturday after that for nearly thirteen years.

Can you imagine how much compromising it took for four different, individual teen-age girls to arrange singing schedules, taste in clothes, hairdos, even the choice of songs—not to mention the harmonies? Who would sing melody? Who would sing the solo line? Believe it or not, after all these years of working together and singing together, the sisters all still truly love each other!

Today they are all married and among the four of them have fourteen children. They still perform and need to make even more compromises, for now their schedules are even more complicated, the sacrifices more difficult.

I asked them once, "How do you do it?"

"We know a lot about harmony," they answered. "And the joy of harmony is that *you can't sing it by yourself.*"

Compromise is not easy. That's why we call it the *toll*-way. But I promise you, if you will pay the "duties" on this road of love, you will find that the journey was well worth the price!

COMPROMISE IS LOWERING YOURSELF

The first "duty" on the *toll*-way is *lowering* yourself to give someone else an opportunity. *Love does not demand its own way!* There can be no community without compromise. You've met people with hardened opinions, iron wills, frozen viewpoints. This stance will only lead to loneliness, for I can assure you that nobody wants to be around people who can only see one point-of-view—theirs!

Frequently, these people mistakenly assume that their unwavering position is a sign of strength. When it comes to moral values, as we saw in chapter seven, that is often true. But many times, this single-minded view of life is nothing more than a disguised stubbornness.

The really *strong* persons are those who have self-denial at the core of their love. They are people who can give of themselves freely. They know how to go more than halfway. They can compromise when the going gets rough. For compromise is self-denial; it is backing down, backing off, and settling for less in the present moment to gain more in the end. Compromising is lowering yourself *only to be lifted.*

Retreating is sometimes the wisest way to advance. Compromise today; make up for it tomorrow. Give a little now. Regain it—and more—down the road. *Compromising is taking one step back in order to take two steps forward.*

I have a friend who claims that the complaint department is really the quality control department. A successful company or person must be humble enough to listen to constructive criticism and then to make creative changes. That's compromising for success. That's lowering yourself only to be lifted. There is a principle I have learned to live by, which I discuss at length in the *Be Happy Attitudes:* "I don't want my own way—I want to do what's right!" Compromising is being willing to lower yourself.

COMPROMISE IS LOOKING BEYOND

The second "duty" on the *toll*-way is *looking*—looking for better ideas, new insights, broader views, brighter ways to help. This way of loving assumes that somebody else knows something you don't know. It is looking beyond the present moment to the big picture. Is there a tension or a problem in your marriage or a relationship? Maybe there is a disagreement between your boss and you? If so, perhaps you need to practice looking at the larger perspective. Compromise your feelings— your hurts, your sense of rejection, and your despair. Forget about them. Compromise is another word for humility.

COMPROMISE IS LIVING WITH THE SPIRIT OF COMMUNITY

The first duty on the *toll*-way of compromise is *lowering* yourself. The second is *looking* to the bigger picture. And the third is *living* with the spirit of community. By that I mean a give-and-take attitude. Compromise is "living" with people, trying to understand and appreciate their ideas, even when you don't share their viewpoints.

Why is America unique among all the nations of the world? *Pluralism.* Every element is represented in this country. All religions are free to practice their faith.

Freedom! That's the trademark of our social fabric. But could this distinct quality also be a weakness? If every religious, ideological, sociological, cultural, ethnic, racial, and sexual group becomes self-centered to the point where "MY RIGHTS!" become more important than the spirit of loving and caring for one another, then we are in danger. "MY RIGHT" loses its MIGHT, when it turns into a FIGHT!

In other words, my freedom loses its moral power if it fails to move forward and outward with love! The plain and simple fact is that no one has a right to demand all of his rights all of the time! So compromise! Give and take! Be a part of a community. Get on the team!

You can imagine how important the art of compromise and a sense of community are when you manage a baseball team. And compromising, like managing, is possible when you can *look* for better ideas, *listen* to what your players are saying, and *live* with them, making room for their viewpoints.

I once asked my good friend Tommy LaSorda, manager of the Los Angeles Dodgers, what contributed to the success of his team. Here's what he said:

> Well, I think a manager has to be a leader, and I have thought a lot about which qualities are important in a manager. I found my answer in church. The priest talked about Solomon, who is the paragon of truth and wisdom. And the Lord went to Solomon and said that He appreciated all that Solomon had done for Him, and He wanted to give him a gift. God said, "Any gift that you would want, I would love to give to you." And Solomon thought a minute and said, "The greatest gift that you can give me is an understanding heart." I think that is one of the real qualities that a manager should have.
>
> You should understand how the players feel. You should understand that when a player pops up with the tying run at third base with less than two outs, no one feels any worse than he does. So if you have an understanding heart, I think you are able to get along a great deal better with your players.

It is no wonder that Tommy has been recognized more than once as manager of the year. He looks for the big picture; he listens to what his players are really feeling; he understands. These traits can't help but build a community spirit. A team will not excel if each member cannot compromise on his personal goals and rights.

Perhaps we can see now what compromise really is! Compromise is:

- *Learning* how to live abundantly, even when you don't get your own way.
- *Listening* to what others are saying and requesting. It is hearing their opinions, their views, and their interpretations—even when you don't agree.
- *Lowering* yourself to give someone else an opportunity.
- *Looking* for better ideas, new insights, broader views, brighter ways to help.
- *Living* with a give-and-take attitude. And it is . . .
- *Letting go!*

LET GO AND LET GOD!

Compromise is letting God have His way in your life. Can't you sense it—that there is a God? That a divine destiny is operating in the universe? That there is a purpose for your life? That God has a road He wants you to walk—a road that will lead to genuine peace and authentic pleasure? Do you need to re-evaluate and review your values and your views and, perhaps, change or convert or compromise your long-held posture or position?

A chief executive officer of a major corporation said to me, "For years I've been motivated by fame and fortune. Now I'm asking myself three questions: (1) What do I really want to accomplish in my life? (2) If I keep living and working the way I am, will I succeed? (3) If I make it—will I really be satisfied and happy in the end?"

Those are three good questions for all of us to ask ourselves! And when you do, be prepared to *let go* if:

A. Your views or your values tear apart your precious human relationships.

B. Your lifestyle causes your faith in God to drift aimlessly, dangerously downstream.

C. Your habits or hobbies threaten your health of body and happiness of spirit.

You must be willing to let go of all disruptive and destructive patterns of thought and behavior.

Yes, compromising is letting God have His way and His will in your life. This may not be what you really want to do! But it is the difference between being moral and immoral. An immoral person is somebody who does what he wants to do, when he wants to do it, the way he wants to do it—whether it is right or wrong. That's immorality. By contrast, morality is doing what is right, even if you don't like it. This is the point beyond which you cannot compromise.

All of which leads us to an important question: "When do we compromise and when don't we?" I want to suggest four times when compromising is the wise choice, the loving choice!

1. Compromise When Your Losses Are Irreversible.

When I returned from Europe some years ago, there was a memo for me to call a friend, Pat Shaughnessy, a pastor in Phoenix, Arizona. The note said he was at a Los Angeles hospital.

I called right away. "What are you doing there?" I asked.

He replied, "I was on my way to Korea, standing at the Pan Am air center, when all of a sudden there was an explosion. Three people were killed. I was closest to the bomb, and suddenly I found myself lying on the floor. My right leg was blown off between the hip and the knee. Blood just gushed out. But I never lost consciousness. My first thought was, *Lord, if I have to go, I'm ready. But I don't want to. I enjoy preaching about*

Jesus so much because Christ is such a wonderful person. My second thought was, *My wife, I hope she won't be too hurt by what is happening to me.* Then, on the way to the hospital, they were pumping blood into me, and it was a mad scene. They said I wouldn't live, and I was wide awake. Then this thought struck me, *I don't need a right leg to preach the gospel!"*

Pat has compromised. He has accepted the loss of a leg. We all always need to look at what we have left, not at what we have lost. We must learn to compromise in the face of a hurt or a loss we cannot change.

Teddy Kennedy has certainly suffered some irreversible losses in his life, yet he has gone on. To help others who have been hurt or are going through agonizing losses, Senator Kennedy shares this poem:

LET IT BE FORGOTTEN

Let it be forgotten,
As a flower is forgotten,
Forgotten as a fire
That once was singing gold.
Let it be forgotten,
For ever and ever—
Time is a kind friend,
He will make us old.

If anyone asks,
Say it was forgotten
Long and long ago—
As a flower,
As a fire,
As a hushed foot-fall
In a long forgotten snow. *

---

*Sara Teasdale, *Collected Poems of Sara Teasdale* (Macmillan: New York, 1966), 135. Reprinted with permission of Macmillan Publishing Company.

If you have suffered an irreversible loss, then be assured of this: Time will make the pain less harsh. It will not go away completely—no more than the memories will ever leave—but the pain will become bearable.

2. Compromise When Your Dignity Has Been Denied.

Compromise when your self-esteem has been scratched, when you, your position, or your performance has not received deserved respect or recognition.

Few people are more unhappy or more miserable than those who lack the humility to overlook personal affronts and insults—obvious or oblique, real or fancied, intentional or unintentional. Several illustrations come to mind.

Albert Schweitzer, the renowned, dedicated man who merited over fifty honorary doctorates, was one of the greatest men of our century. He built his hospital in what was then the Belgian Congo, and the natives normally would do anything for him. But one day when he needed to build a wall, he asked one tribal native to carry some wood. The native, who was busy reading a book, said, "I am sorry, Doctor, but I'm an intellectual now; I'm busy reading and intellects don't carry wood!" Dr. Schweitzer replied, "Well, I congratulate you! I always wanted to be an intellectual, but I never succeeded, so I'll carry the wood!" And he did!

At the height of the Civil War, Abraham Lincoln wondered how the war was going. Rather than ask General McClellan to come to the White House and report, he decided that he and the secretary of war would go to the general's house in the battle area. They made their way to the general's home and waited. Finally the general came in, walked right on upstairs to his room, and never acknowledged the president and the secretary. They thought he'd be back in a minute with cleaner garb, but he didn't return. They asked the maid to go upstairs and check on the general.

When she came down she was aghast! "I'm sorry, Mr. President," she said, "but he said to me, 'Tell President Lincoln I'm tired and that I've gone to bed.'"

The secretary of war said to Lincoln, "Surely you're not going to let him get by with that? You will relieve him, will you not?"

The president thought about it for a long time and, finally, when he broke the silence, said, "No, I will not relieve him. That man wins battles, and I would hold his horse and clean his shoes if it would hasten the end of this bloodshed by one hour."

Doesn't that remind you of Jesus Christ? He overheard His followers talking behind His back. "When Jesus is gone, who is going to be the top man here? You, Peter, you, John, or Thomas?" Do you know what Jesus did? He asked for a basin of water and a towel. And before they shared the first communion, He got down and started to wash their feet.

"Wait a minute," Peter said. "I should wash your feet. You shouldn't wash mine." But Jesus just moved from person to person and washed their dirty feet and wiped them with a towel.

You compromise if you teach somebody a lesson by helping them when you do not have to. Schweitzer hauled wood, Lincoln would have held the man's horse. Jesus washed the disciples' feet. Great men have revealed their greatness by showing when to help, to bow, to compromise.

3. Compromise When You're Wrong—But Too Proud to Admit It!

Some of the hardest words to speak are the same words that lead to joy and peace. These hard but happy words are: "You were right! I was wrong!"

How can you salvage your self-esteem when your pride has been shipwrecked on the rocks of a wrong decision? By proudly proclaiming yourself to be a normal, imperfect, yet loveable human being through statements like these:

- "I made a mistake!"
- "Forgive me."
- "Allow me to correct myself."
- "Thank you for permitting me the freedom to improve my position."
- "Thank you for respecting my right to correct myself."
- "I am honored that you would allow me the privilege of compromising my viewpoint in light of the growth I am experiencing now."

When your pride has been wounded because your position has been faulted, you can rescue your self-esteem by openness and honesty. So, when confession leads to compromise, your dignity is immediately nourished by your honesty. You are honored by your humility. You have extracted positive possibilities from your predicament.

In old England, when a man was to be knighted, the queen or the king tapped each shoulder with a sword, and he was declared to be a knight. But there's one thing every potential knight had to do: He had to be humble, to kneel, to bow, to compromise his pride. He had to kneel to be knighted.

Yes, compromise can be kingly! Your life can be crowned with joy and happiness if you discover the peace and the pleasantness that proceeds out of the heart of a humble person.

Compromise: I am knighted with honor and glory when I compromise *my* right in the face of *what's* right!

4. Compromise When the Rewards Are Heavenly—But the Price Is Horrific!

In explaining this principle, no life is more inspiring, illuminating, and illustrative than the life of Jesus Christ. And no single event in the life of Jesus stands out as dramatically as the crucial experience that occurred in the Garden of Gethsemane the night before Jesus was crucified.

The scene begins at supper. The twelve apostles are sharing a Passover meal with Jesus. Judas slips out to prepare to betray his Master. Jesus now leads His followers out into the garden to pray. He moves quietly into a secluded section where He can commune with God. He is fully aware that if He doesn't turn now, run away, escape, tonight He will be betrayed and tomorrow He will be crucified.

He is young, only 33 years old! He is alive! He has so much to live for! To stay in the garden will mean capture and crucifixion! Now comes the prayer of all prayers. Hear Him: ". . . Father, all things are possible for You. Take this cup away from Me; nevertheless, not what I will, but what You will" (Mark 14:36).

What visions now pass through His mind? Does He see millions, hundreds of millions, yes, a billion believers two thousand years down the road who will respect and reverence Him for His courage, His commitment, and His cross? Does He see the untold hundreds of millions of souls saved because of His sacrifice and His death? Does this heavenly reward prove enough to move Him to pay the horrific price?

This we know—He compromised His will to fulfill God's dream! The result? Betrayal. Trial before Pilate. Scourging in the morning. Crucifixion at noon. Death at mid-day Friday. But new life on Sunday! And today He is Lord over a kingdom of untold millions who share His life and His love.

Compromise can be kingly!

THE ROAD OF LOVE:
CONSIDER TAKING THE *SUB*-WAY!

Real Love Forgives and Forgets

"Love is not . . . resentful."
1 Corinthians 13:5

"Forgive *and* forget! That's impossible!"

She was actually angry at hearing my advice! "Impossible! Impossible!" she repeated. She was a hurting woman, a relatively innocent victim of a cruel divorce. Her self-esteem was shattered. She was bitter—understandably so.

"Let's discuss it," I offered.

"I doubt if I can *forgive,*" she finally volunteered. "*Forget?* No way!"

"But it is possible," I repeated. "Listen . . ." She was listening, so I continued. "Let me ask you a question: Is it possible you are confusing reconciliation with forgiveness?"

There followed one of the longest pauses I have experienced in my years of pastoral counseling. "Forgiveness does not mean you have to approve his behavior! You could never do that! But forgiveness does mean you are going to put it behind you—and, yes—in practical terms—forget it! Which means you'll bury the hatchet and not leave the handle above the ground! But to forgive and forget does not mean you have to have a restored relationship! You don't even need to become friends. You just have to stop being enemies!"

Her whole body seemed to breathe a heavy sigh, and her face seemed to lose ten years of age! She suddenly relaxed, looking enormously relieved of a colossal burden! The turnaround had begun! Healing love was moving in. Result? She salvaged the respect and love of the rest of her close friends and family, for they were becoming tired of her morbid, negative, unhappy side! Had she not learned to forgive and forget, the rest of her meaningful relationships could have been hopelessly poisoned and destroyed. The alternative to forgiveness is destruction beyond calculation.

Any fool can count the seeds in an apple, but only God can count the apples in one seed. The principle works with bad seeds, bad feelings, and bad thoughts just as it works with good seeds, good feelings, and good thoughts!

"I am going to choose to forgive! To let love come back!" she promised. Result? Several years later, she attracted a wonderful husband! Today her life is precious, glorious, and beautiful! More amazingly, she said to me recently, "Dr. Schuller, I ran into my ex-husband. And guess what—I didn't hate him anymore! The resentment is gone. My feelings are kind and pleasant." This all happened when she chose a positive attitude! You can, too!

Robert Frost once suggested that before we build walls, we should make sure we know what we're walling out and what we're walling in.

No wall is more impenetrable, more formidable than the wall of resentment. This silent killer of relationships is a common cause of divorce, split friendships, and broken partnerships.

So when relationships break up and the "traffic backs up," go *under* the wall of resentment. Take the *sub*-way to forgiveness.

REMEDIES FOR RESENTMENT

The Apostle Paul says, "Love is not . . . resentful." That sounds noble, but in practical terms how do you handle the person whose lifestyle, whose behavior, or whose attitude toward you meets with your nonapproval? How do you handle the nonapprovable persons, experiences, or situations?

You have several options. At the shallowest level of

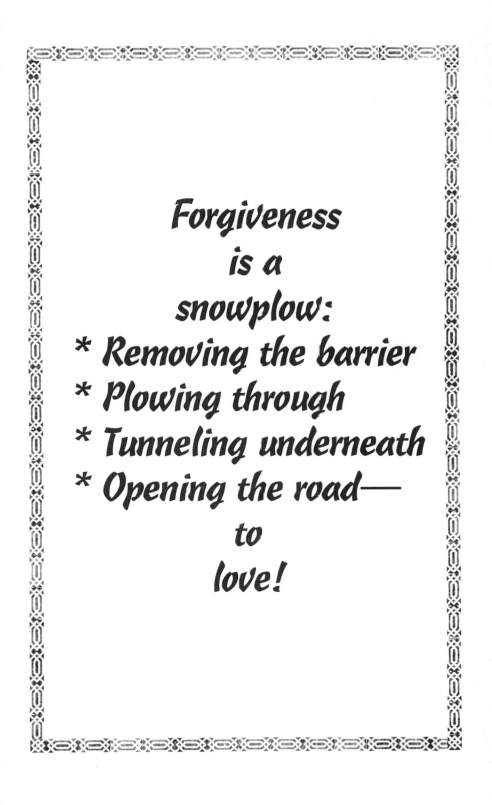

Forgiveness
is a
snowplow:
* Removing the barrier
* Plowing through
* Tunneling underneath
* Opening the road—
to
love!

nonapproval there is what I would call *reticence*, which means there's a silence about the whole situation or the person. You simply avoid the issue if possible. For example, in a meeting where someone has become angry and is ripping into another person, you might be quiet, wait for a pause, then abruptly change the subject.

The second reaction, a little more intense, is operating when you understand exactly what's happening and rather than avoid all confrontation through reticence you try *resistance*.

Instead of ignoring a tense situation, you may stiffen up and bristle within. But you want to do anything you can to try to keep yourself protected from an involvement with the "obnoxious" person. You hope the conversation can be terminated swiftly, perhaps even gracefully. But deep within yourself you've already made a judgment; you have your mind made up. You are disturbed by this person and the situation is now brimming with problems, obstacles, and difficulties. Reticence has been replaced by a more intense form of inner resistance.

There is also a third reaction, which is even more intense— *retreat*. In the setting of this tense meeting, you'll probably say to yourself, *Hey, I want to get out of here! And as quickly as possible!* You may make an excuse to split, or you may stop attending the meetings. You may even quit going to the organization, the church, or whatever it is. In a marriage, retreat may mean separation.

Sometimes, even though you long to walk away from a person or situation, retreat simply isn't an available option. You find yourself trapped. You're reticent, you're resistant, you want to retreat but you can't, and you'll probably react with the fourth level of nonapproval, and that's *rebellion*. This means, in the meeting I've described, you may interrupt the angry person and begin lambasting him for the way he is attacking the other person, the result often being an argument.

Rebellion is often expressed verbally, but it takes other forms as well. We all have our own instinctive or contrived, subconscious or conscious ways of rebelling, such as in our dress—consider the "hippies" of the 1960s and the "punkers" of the 1980s.

Nonapproval at its most negative level will result in *resentment*. Reticence? You can ignore it. Resistance? You can just play it away. Retreat? Take off! Rebellion? Get angry, verbally abuse someone, thumb your nose at authority! Resentment is the most dangerous reaction to a nonapproving experience or situation or person. It is the most dangerous because it is self-destructive. It is anger turned inward, outward, upward, and downward—all at the same time.

Question: Are you carrying resentments? How many fears, how many anxieties, how many worries are you suffering from because you will not forgive somebody who hurt you deeply? How many sunny days are turned gray by your angry mind— seething, quarreling in fantasy bouts with your adversary, who may be an ex-husband, an ex-wife, a relative, a neighbor, a customer, a client, or a clerk? Are you depressed and unhappy or even suffering from ulcers, high blood pressure, or heart problems because you will not forgive?

Next question: Are you developing wrinkles on your face that will become permanent creases, monuments to the fact that you spent most of your life thinking angry thoughts that twisted your expression into a permanent frown?

Last question: How many friends did you once have who no longer talk to you because you have developed a reputation of pouting, grumbling, and complaining?

This reminds me of the story of the monk who went to a monastery on a mountain in Spain. One of the requirements of this monastic order was that each monk must maintain perpetual silence. Only after two years was a monk allowed to speak, and then only two words. This was followed by two additional years of silence, two more words, and so on.

A young initiate had spent his first two years at the monastery and was called by his superior to make his first two-word statement. He said, "Bed hard." Two years passed. He got his second chance. His next two words were, "Food bad." Two more years passed. His next words were: "I quit!"

The superior looked at him and said: "It doesn't surprise me. All you've done since you got here is complain, complain, complain!"

This story brings a smile, but in all seriousness, none of us wants to go through life bearing the reputation of a grumbling, complaining, resentful person.

At one time or another all of us will face a situation that will "make our blood boil." We will find ourselves justifiably or unjustifiably angry. Yet Paul says that "Love is not resentful." What in the world can he possibly mean? An illustration from my childhood may help explain his meaning. Born and raised in northwest Iowa, I vividly recall the feelings of winter's first snow. The sight of snowflakes was wonderful. What we didn't appreciate were the blizzards, because these storms, fueled by driving winds of fifty to sixty miles an hour, often piled snow so high in drifts that the roads were impassable. We were marooned, unable to drive to the store and buy food. It was serious. One positive thing—there always is *something* positive—I did not have to go to school! When the storm ended I remember looking out of our farm house, half a mile down the road, to the hill where we could see the snowplow coming, cutting through the drifts, slicing the snow, chopping it up and blowing it in a huge, spewing stream into a ditch. After the snowplow came through, the road was open again, and we could go for our food. And I was obligated to return to my education.

Resentments are like snowdrifts, and forgiveness acts like the snowplow. Forgiveness, in the eyes of the non-Christian, is simply a matter of passive acquittal. But to the Christian, that's not it at all. Forgiveness is the snowplow, opening the road, removing the barrier, plowing through, or tunneling underneath, so that communication can be resumed and what people are trying to say can be heard again. We dialog and interchange; we move back and forth. Whether it's between God and myself or a person and myself, forgiveness is a snowplow.

We all make many mistakes. We all say things we do not mean and forget to say the things we should. Consequently, a lot of resentments can build up in just a day.

How do you handle them? We've shown how *reticence, retreat, rebellion,* or *resentment* don't work. Now let me give you the Christian option: *Repentance* and *forgiveness.*

In digging under the wall of resentments, in seeking sincerely to forgive, we are bound to run into some obstacles. After all, even a mighty snowplow will be slowed by huge snowdrifts. It's the same with Christian forgiveness.

Obstacle #1: An Extreme Sense of Injustice

Odds are that if you're basically a decent person and yet are plagued by resentments, you probably feel you have been treated unfairly or thoroughly victimized. Your overpowering respect for justice gives birth to this resentment. Resentment, in a perverse fashion, becomes your way to mete out justice. That's not right. The Bible says, "'Vengeance is Mine. I will repay,' says the Lord" (Rom. 12:19).

That's that. At no point in the Bible does God ever command the Christian to execute that kind of justice against sins. He reserves the right to execute vengeance. We have to trust that He can do so in many ways that we cannot. In fact, we must trust that He is already executing justice.

I have often been helped by the biblical story of Joseph. He was sold by his brothers and became a slave in Egypt. The brothers had hoped they could kill him and get him out of the way. Instead he became a ruler. Hoping to kill him, they ended up through the providence of God crowning him. By the time he saw them again Joseph was able to say, "You meant evil against me; but God meant it for good" (Gen. 50:20).

Let justice be handled by the Lord. He knows how to take care of people. You can be sure that if you have been truly victimized, the person who has victimized you is already paying the price in his own conscience or heart or mind. You may say, "But, Dr. Schuller, I don't see any evidence of that."

Trust God. He has His own ways of executing justice. He is doing it. He can, He is, He will do a much better job of it than you or I can.

May those around us that we love be spared when we try to take justice into our own hands. God have mercy on your wife or your husband or your kids! I never have met a person whose personal form of executing justice changed him into a joyous, happy, beautiful human being in the process!

A man who was the victim of injustice once said to his pastor, "But wouldn't it be *man*-like of me to be angry?"

The pastor replied, "Indeed it would. But it would be *Christ*-like of you to forgive."

Obstacle #2: Exaggerating Negative Experiences

We tend to emphasize the little negative events of life that get under our skin, and we forget all the little positive events of life that should fill us with joy, hope, and love. Any person who has hurt you does have many fine qualities, but chances are you can't see them. That's because we are all by nature negative thinkers. We see the wrong, and we don't see the good. That becomes an obstacle. We take a little detail and get hung up on it.

An artist was teaching his students how to paint. On a special occasion, he took them on an all-day trip to a particular hill where the sunsets were exceptionally beautiful. Just as the colors broke—purple, red, pink, orange, yellow, and gold—the teacher walked behind his students who were all intently capturing the artistic moment. To his disappointment he found one student who was diligently painting the shingle on a barn in the valley under the sunset. He had missed the glorious shading of sunset in favor of a shingle!

What's the point? Don't use a microscope to find the negative when if you'll just open your eyes you will be overwhelmed by a whole landscape of positive!

Obstacle #3: Ignoring the Positive Possibilities in Negative Experiences

Every situation has some positive element in it. No person is totally bad. No situation is entirely hopeless.

I used to give lectures in which I took a piece of paper and drew a circle on it. Then I drew a straight line, and next to it added a curving line. I tacked the paper up and asked the class to tell me what they saw. The reactions were interesting.

"I see a straight line."

"I see a curve."

"I see a circle."

Some saw the objects and turned them into a work of art into which they read all kinds of meaning. In the process, many of them committed little Freudian slips, I suppose, but the point was that *no* student ever said, "I see a piece of paper!"

All they saw were the black marks! They saw the negatives; they didn't see the positives. Our first inclination in a potentially nonapproving situation is to see the negative and not the positive.

I shall never forget the night Mrs. Schuller and I were on the East Coast in a very prominent city where I was to deliver the Sunday message in a huge church the next morning. I had just come from an international trip only a few hours before. At the Geneva airport I had cashed two $50 traveler's checks and received two $50 bills in exchange.

I was preparing for my sermon in a hotel when I noticed that a particular movie was playing in the neighborhood theater. I had reason to believe the movie would give me some good sermon illustrations, so Arvella and I went to the theater. We stood in line, a long line, and after checking our watches we knew the movie was about to start. I didn't want to miss the opening, and at just two minutes before the scheduled starting time we arrived at the box office. I slid my $50 bill through the slot and the ticket teller passed back the two tickets. Then she paused, looked at the bill, and said, "I'm sorry. We don't take $50 bills."

"You can't reject it!" I said. "Do you know what that bill says? 'This is legal tender for all debts public and private.' You can't refuse it!"

"I'm sorry. We can't take it."

Now, never in my life have I been a public protester, but the line was getting longer and longer behind me, and it was beginning to drizzle. "I'm sure you can take it because it's a good $50 bill," I pleaded.

"I'm sorry. We *won't* take it."

The people behind us glared. I could feel the impatience of the crowd. Finally, the ticket teller said, "You've got your tickets."

"All right," I answered. "Thank you." And I walked in.

Suddenly, the ticket girl stuck her head out of the box office and yelled at the head usher, "That man didn't pay!"

I thought, *Oh, my gosh! I hope nobody recognizes me!*

The usher stopped me and asked, "What's the big idea!"

"She wouldn't take my $50 bill, and it's all I've got! I just left Geneva twelve hours ago, and I'm sorry. But watch where I sit, and you just check with the hotel and see if there is a Robert Schuller listed. Check out if they think he's honest or not. By the time I leave the theater, you'll have had time to check me out."

Unfortunately, halfway through the movie I had to step out to the rest room. I no sooner got in the men's room than there was that same usher! "O.K.," he said, "you are either a counterfeiter or the greatest con man I've ever met."

"Did you check the hotel?" I questioned.

"No!" he said sternly. "I don't have to. I can spot a con man a mile off."

"Look," I said, reaching for my billfold. "Here is the $50 bill. You take it, check it out, and when I leave the theater, give me $40 back, please. I want to go in and finish watching the movie." And I left him with the $50 bill.

When the movie was over and Arvella and I walked out, I couldn't find the usher. But I did see a man in a black coat who looked "official," so I said to him, "I'm looking for the head usher. He's got my $50 bill."

He looked at me with a frown and said, "Oh, so you're the guy with the $50 bill! We *don't take* $50 bills here."

"Well, I want my change, $40, or I want my $50 bill back," I persisted.

He reached into his pocket and with a hateful look on his face said, "Here is your blankety-blank $50 bill," and threw it on the floor.

I reached down, picked it up, and put it in my pocket. Do you know what? I was mad!

We walked out of the theater, and it was raining. We were three blocks from the hotel. Arvella said, "Bob, this is a great opportunity to practice what you preach. This situation is loaded with possibilities."

Frankly, I didn't feel like practicing what I preach. At that moment I did not even feel like preaching. I certainly didn't feel like looking for the possibilities. "Yeah? Like what?" I asked.

"Well, let's go back to the hotel, break the $50 bill, return to the theater, and pay them what we owe them. Then the usher will listen to a witness for Jesus Christ."

Suddenly, my resentment was plowed through. The possibility of sharing Christ's love overcame any anger I had felt. "O.K. Let's do it!"

We walked to the hotel, got the change for the $50 bill, and hurried back to the theater. We stood in the rain at the locked door and knocked persistently until the girl who ran the snack bar let us in. "Not you again?" she said.

"Please, may I see the head usher?" I asked.

Just then I saw the usher coming down the steps carrying his tuxedo. He was wearing his street clothes. "Oh, my God," he said, "not you again?"

"Yes, it is I again. I have come to pay you the $10 I owe you."

"Oh, you didn't have to do that," he said.

"Yes, I did." I said with a smile. "I owe it to you, and I want you to know that I am doing this for one reason: I claim to be a Christian, and it's very exciting trying to follow Christ in daily life. I want you—if you ever hear people say that 'Christians are all a bunch of hypocrites, that there's nothing to this Jesus Christ, and there's nothing to this God business'—I want you never to forget that there was once a man who came in dripping wet from a walk in the rain to pay his $10 because he was a Christian."

The usher's eyes were moist. He took the $10 and said, "Yes, sir. Thank you, sir. Good night, sir. I'm very sorry."

We smiled and shook hands.

To forgive doesn't mean that you erase the slate. Forgiveness means that you cut the road open, you dig under the wall, you move back and forth, and you love someone again! You don't just acquit the person. You see the possibilities and make them into something beautiful.

Obstacle #4: Blinding Ourselves to the Positive Possiblities in Negative People

If you know someone who you cannot *like,* much less *love,* then remember: You are not alone!

As Frank Laubach, a great missionary statesman of the 20th century once said: "None of us loves perfectly, but Christ loves perfectly. No human being is totally perfect in love, but Christ is. Now, let's suppose you run into somebody you can't love. What do you do? Do you let yourself hate them? No. Do you tell yourself, 'I'm a Christian; therefore I'm going to love them.' *Yes!* Even though *it might not work,* don't surrender to your negative thoughts about the person. Of course not. You call in the expert, the authority—Jesus Christ."

Here's how Frank taught me to handle such a situation: "Put one hand up in the air, open your palm, and stretch out the other hand with a pointed finger aimed at your adversary. Now pray: 'Jesus Christ, You are perfect love. I am imperfect love. Because I'm imperfect I can't love that guy.' (Keep your finger pointed right at him! Aim at his heart!) 'Jesus Christ, will You please fall into the palm of my hand, flow down through my arm, through my elbow, through my shoulder, my chest, my heart, down my other arm, out of the end of my finger, and hit him, please? Hit him hard! Hit him gently! Hit him beautifully! You love him, Jesus! You can do it! I can't do it! But *You* can!'"

I explained Frank's method some years ago at the Crystal Cathedral. One man who heard me thought to himself, *Boy, Schuller's getting carried away again.* A week later he told me what had happened:

Monday morning I went to work remembering your sermon of the day before. The first person I saw coming into my store was the one salesman I could not stand. I saw him drive up to the curb and get out of his car. I was already in a bad mood. My secretary, who also goes to this church and had heard the same sermon, said to me, "Maybe you'd better try what Dr. Schuller talked about yesterday. Shoot him with prayers."

So before he got in I reached one hand in the air and with the other hand I pointed at him through the window. He was gawking at me as if I were nuts. (Later on he told me he thought I was going to change a light bulb!) But I was praying silently, *Jesus, I can't love that guy. But You can. Flow into my hand, through my arm, through my heart, and You love him, Jesus.*

The most amazing thing happened! I couldn't believe it. The man came up to me and said, "Good morning. How are you today?" I'd never heard him say it that way before. I looked at his face and saw that it had a countenance I'd never seen before. His eyes, that had always looked so nasty, now looked so sweet. It had worked! *I ended up loving this guy!*

A love that forgives casts out all kinds of negative forces. Christ's love can even tunnel under the obstacle of dislike. With Christ's love, it *is* possible to love—even the unloveable! It is possible to forgive—even the unforgivable!

Tragically, the daughter of Jim and Catherine Coyer was brutally murdered. The young man Michael, who killed Debbie, had grown up in the same small town, so he was no stranger. He was found guilty and sentenced to prison.

Five years after Debbie's death, Jim and Catherine moved to California and became members of the Crystal Cathedral. They met with me one afternoon and shared with me their story. Then Jim pulled out a letter and said, "Doctor Schuller, this was written from our heart."

I was so struck by the power of forgiveness and the immensity of love that was exhibited in this letter that I asked then if they would let me use it in a book. Generously, they agreed.

Dear Michael,

The words that follow are going to be the most difficult ones I have attempted to write. I have thought over them many times in the past, but never had the courage to put them on paper. Michael, I want you to know that I, with the help of our Lord Jesus Christ, do forgive you for the act which has so drastically changed our lives. The vacuum and the hurt still are very apparent and felt daily.

Debbie is still missed by many. Please understand that the act itself is the most abhorrent one possible, but because all of us are children of God, it is my Christian duty to forgive. Because I myself would want to be forgiven. Know that God loves you, and thus I love you as a brother in Christ.

In Christ,
James Coyer

No matter how obstinate the obstacle or how horrific the hurt—forgiveness is possible! It's really true, "I can do all things through Christ who strengthens me" (Phil. 4:13).

THE ROAD OF LOVE:
THE *HIGH*-WAY TO THE *GREAT* WAY!

Real Love Believes the Best

"Love . . . believes all things."
     1 Corinthians 13:7

Have you ever been to the Dallas-Fort Worth airport? The roads that loop around the enormous, sprawling complex resemble high-speed highways. They are miles long and very confusing. On one of these loops, about two miles from the terminal I needed, all of a sudden, the rental car I was riding in stopped. So did my heart, for when I looked at my watch, I saw that in sixteen minutes our plane would take off. I couldn't let that happen, so I turned to my associate, Fred Southard, and said, "This is ridiculous. We *cannot* be stopped by a dead car! Come on!"

I opened the door, stuck my hand out, and put my thumb up like a hitchhiker. Amazingly, the first car that came by stopped. "Quick Fred, get in!" I said.

Fred grabbed the suitcases, I grabbed my briefcase and the tuxedos, and both of us ran across six lanes of traffic, carefully dodging the other cars and buses.

I am sure it must have been an interesting sight to see us galloping across the Dallas-Fort Worth highway. I opened the front door of the waiting car. The front seat was occupied by an empty child restraint seat. The back seat was covered with boxes, toys, and other items, but Fred squeezed in. I handed the luggage to him. The lovely young woman who was driving didn't even look to see who we were. She had impetuously, impulsively decided to help someone in trouble.

Thinking she might be frightened, seeing that two men were

221

climbing into her car, I said, "You can trust me. My name is Dr. Schuller."

She looked at me for the first time. Her eyes got wide! "Robert Schuller? You can't be!" she said. "You can't be Dr. Robert Schuller. Not hitchhiking on the Dallas-Fort Worth freeway! You can't be! I don't believe it! *Nobody* will believe it!"

"I am Robert Schuller!"

"If I tell anybody that I picked you up hitchhiking on the freeway today, nobody will believe it," she said, shaking her head.

"Oh, yes, they will. What's your name?"

"Joanne."

By then, she was staring at me and starting to run onto the curb.

"Just watch the road!" I said. Then I opened my briefcase and pulled out my newest book. Before handing it to her, I wrote, "To Joanne, I love to give people a lift myself."

I do love to give people a lift! I love to lift them to *faith* even when there's no apparent reason to believe. I love to lift them with *hope* even when others say, "Give up!" I love to lift them in *love* when they've been hurt.

It's all summed up in the verse in 1 Corinthians 13: "Love . . . believes all things" (v. 7). It's the "faith-hope-love" way to live: The *high*-way of life! And believe me, it's the way to go when you get hurt, when the bottom falls out of a marriage, when you are tempted to turn back and quit on love.

"I was the last to know," a woman said to me. "I feel like such a fool! Everybody knew he was betraying me—except me! I believed him! But that's the last time! I'm never going to believe anyone again!"

She wiped her eyes, squared her shoulders, and looked at me. I saw a hint of a cold, protective gleam in her eye. That scared me, for if she allowed a defensive shell to grow around her heart, she would certainly be doomed to a lonely life.

"You say you were a fool for believing in your husband," I

said, "but I say you made the smart choice, the choice to believe. As for me, I would much rather choose to err on the side of love than on the side of suspicion. I would far rather err on the side of faith than doubt, on the side of grace than retaliation. It's better to have loved and lost than never to have loved at all."

Suddenly, the cold gleam melted. A smile softened her hardened face. "Really?" she said. "I never thought of it that way. I guess I'm O.K. I guess I'm not a fool after all."

I never heard what the outcome for her marriage was, but one thing I am certain of—she chose to believe in love again! When she was tempted to turn her back on love, she chose to take the *high*-way, the way of love—regardless of the outcome.

The *high*-way of love is a love that believes the best!

LOVE BELIEVES THE BEST!

When it comes to other people or any situation in life, we can assume the worst or we can assume the best. Most of us prefer to live safely and suspiciously. We assume the worst so we will be prepared when we hit rock bottom. We pride ourselves on being aware, alert to people who could take advantage of us:

- "Nobody's gonna pull the wool over my eyes!"
- "I'm nobody's fool!"

And so we live life looking over our shoulders, never really trusting anyone.

First Corinthians, however, recommends an alternate route. St. Paul suggests a love that believes the best about those we love; it is a love that jumps to *positive* conclusions. This is faith in others, and faith in love lifts us to the *high*-way of life!

Love without faith is meaningless. It is as flat, dead, and lifeless as a fallen soufflé—the opposite of a perfect soufflé—the delicate baked custard that rises like a golden cloud above its baking dish. I must admit—I have a "thing" about soufflés!

Some years ago in a spiritual experience, God said to me, "Schuller, in order to keep your body healthy, you have to run every day." And then He told me to eat right. For me that meant no cakes, pies, ice cream, breads, or butter. The only desserts my conscience would allow me were fresh fruits and baked soufflés. I reasoned that soufflés were so rare I wouldn't have to worry.

Soon after I went into a restaurant and ordered a soufflé, but they had never heard of one! I found out that only French restaurants serve them, so I immediately started picking out French restaurants. But I found that many of them did not bake soufflés, either. "God has a fantastic sense of humor," I laughed. "That's why he lets me eat soufflés—I can't find them!"

Recently, when Mrs. Schuller and I were returning from a ministry in Australia, we stopped over in Hawaii, and I began to prepare my Sunday sermon. I had what I thought was an inspiration for a great illustration in the message I was writing. We would find a French restaurant where I could order a soufflé. I planned to create a sermon illustration around this soufflé!

Arvella and I arrived at the restaurant and were seated at a quiet corner table. The waiter handed us the menu. A few minutes later he returned and asked if we were ready to order. Now, if you are going to order a baked soufflé, you have to order at the beginning of the meal because it does take a while to bake. I said to the waiter, "We'll begin by ordering our dessert. We will both have a soufflé."

"Oh," he exclaimed, "but we don't bake soufflés!"

Stunned, I said, "Of course you bake soufflés! I'm told this restaurant makes the best soufflés in Hawaii!"

"I'm sorry," he replied. "We don't bake soufflés."

"Please check," I begged. So he left and came back after a few minutes. "I'm sorry. We no longer bake soufflés."

"That can't be," I lamented. "This is very important to me. Please go back to the chef and ask him if he'll make us a soufflé. I know he can."

By this time the waiter was a little flushed, but he left again only to return and say, "I'm awfully sorry, but the kitchen is not making soufflés today."

I grasped the medal I wear around my neck and began to read aloud: *When faced with a mountain, I will not quit. I will keep on striving . . . .* May I talk to the *maitre d'*?" I pleaded.

"Yes," he answered and left.

The maitre d' was at our table immediately. He was a handsome, charming, debonair gentleman. "Sir," I explained, "we've come a long way just for a soufflé."

"I'm sorry, sir," he replied. "We can't make a soufflé for you."

I tried a different approach. "Look, I am desperately in need of anecdotal material. You see, I write books and talk on television. And I came to your restaurant specifically to get an illustration—all about a soufflé. Please, may I talk to the executive chef?"

The maitre d' threw up his hands. "Just a moment!"

Pretty soon, into the crowded dining room strode the executive chef, clad in a tall white hat and apron. He came right up to our table and stopped short. Suddenly his mouth dropped open, his eyes widened with the "I-know-you-I-see-you-on-television" look, and he said, "*Father* Schuller! What a surprise! I never miss you on television! So you're the one who's been asking for the soufflé!"

"Yes," I answered, "like only you can bake it!"

"I'll bake you a good soufflé!" he said.

We selected our entrée, and as we were finishing our meal, the chef himself entered and paraded through the crowded, gorgeous dining room, holding high a huge platter draped with beautiful napkins, covering two masterful soufflés! Golden toasted brown! They rose high out of their individual ceramic dishes like small, steaming, feather-light, upside-down angel food cakes! And to top it all the maitre d' announced: "Compliments of the house!"

There is no dessert quite like a baked soufflé! A good soufflé is like a bud that has opened to full bloom! Like a symphony with all instruments in a final massive chord of glorious harmony! Like seeing a person come out and blossom under the magic spell of *love*! Yes, "love is the soufflé of life!" *Faith gives love its life and life its lift!* I made these points in my next sermon.

There is nothing that can match a person whose life has risen to beautiful new possibilities for joy and happiness because of loving faith.

As a child I used to sing the old hymn, "Love lifted me . . . when nothing else could help, Love lifted me!" When you believe the best about others, when trust, admiration, and esteem are at the core of your attitudes, then miracles will happen!

LOVE THAT BELIEVES THE BEST— REMOVES THE WEIGHT OF DOUBT!

What is it that weighs us down?

- Suspicion!
- Doubt!
- Fear!

These negative defenses hold us down and keep us from experiencing full, rich, rewarding love relationships. They hang over us like a cloud, blocking out the possibilities of love, keeping us from being happy, from loving, from being loved!

"Perfect love casts out fear." We've all heard this Scripture verse. But what in the world did the writer, John, mean when he said, "*Perfect* love"?

Well, I contend that none of us is perfect. But when we make a mistake, when we fail, the best way to correct the situation is to *believe* that life is not over and *have the faith* to try again.

In the same way "perfect" love is a love that has faith at its foundation. This faith can cut through the chain of fear that imprisons our heart. It can clear away the clouds of doubt and let the love shine through.

On one Valentine's Day I married a lovely young couple at a hotel in a distant city. After the wedding the four of us who had participated in the ceremony sat down with the couple in the hotel restaurant and shared the wedding cake with them. The young bride then opened her purse and said, "Dr. Schuller, I have a special gift for your wife. It's my way of saying thank you for marrying us."

Into my hand she placed a little jade elephant about an inch and a half long from the tip of its trunk to the tip of its tail. Around the two front feet of the little charm was a tiny golden chain.

"This little elephant symbolizes what my faith has done for me," she said. "I have been liberated from the terrible thoughts I had about myself and now see the beautiful possibilities God has for me and those I love."

She went on to remind me of how mighty elephants are controlled. Once a wild elephant is captured, the captors tie the end of a long chain around the elephant's foot. The other end is tied to a huge banyan tree.

The great elephant will pull with all its strength, but it can't budge the banyan tree. Finally, after struggling for days and weeks, when the elephant barely lifts its ponderous foot and feels the chain tightening, it drops its foot heavily to the ground because it knows that further struggle is useless. The elephant has surrendered to the chain.

At this point the trainers know the elephant is really trapped forever. For when they take the elephant and chain it to a little iron stake by a circus tent, the elephant never attempts to pull away because it still thinks it is chained to a banyan tree.

You are not chained to a banyan tree! Your problem is not insurmountable! You can repair and redeem a broken relationship if you will dare to cut through the chains of fear.

Face it—life will be dominated either by love and trust or by suspicion and doubt.

So, take a leap of faith. Dare to believe in others. Be a lifter, and you will find to your amazement that you, in turn, are lifted. You always feel great when you have helped someone. Love puts back what you give out. A believing love takes away the weights of doubt and gives you wings of faith.

LOVE THAT BELIEVES THE BEST—GIVES LIFTING POWER UNDER THE WINGS OF FAITH!

When you take the *high*-way of faith, hope, and love, suddenly you are lifted above the problems, fears, and doubts. You have discovered a new perspective! You can see possibilities! You can imagine new solutions! You can anticipate happy endings! You become a possibility thinker and begin to practice the uplifting power of possibilitizing!

Doubt Blinds You To Possibilities!
But Faith Opens Your Eyes To New Opportunities!

Possibilitizing is *imagining*, it is *visualizing*, it is *praying*, it is *multiplying* mentally, it is *overcoming*, it is *anticipating*—in spite of the problems you encounter.

Possibilitizing Is Imagining

Positive love will overpower the negative thoughts, so you will be able to possibilitize your way out of a tough situation by imagining that things are going to get better.

While lecturing in New York, I placed a telephone call to a young woman who told me how helpful the "Hour of Power" ministry had been to her. She told me, "A year ago I had major surgery, and it didn't look like I'd live. Your positive messages reinforced what my doctor was telling me. When I asked him, 'Do you think I'll ever walk again?' he looked at me intently and said, 'That's the wrong question. The right question is not do *I* think you'll ever walk again, but do *you* think you'll ever walk again?'"

Problems really have become serious when they distract your eyes from the goal. Constantly imagine that things are going to get better for you and the ones you love. Situations will not stay the way they are. If you imagine they're going to get better, you will be in a frame of mind to contribute to their getting better.

Possibilitizing Is Visualizing

You must see the victory beyond the battle of the hour, see the ultimate reward instead of the pain, see the crown instead of the cross.

For years swimmer Steve Genter from Lakewood, California, trained for the Munich Olympics. He wanted to win so badly the 200-meter freestyle race. You may know what happened. One week before the big event his lung collapsed. The doctors said that would wipe him out, but Steve didn't agree. He looked beyond the moment. At his insistence surgeons cut his chest open, repaired the lung, and stitched him back up. When names were called for the event in Munich, Steve Genter stepped forward, his chest taped and stitched!

The starter fired his gun and Steve dove in. He was in the 100-meter turn of the 200-meter freestyle, in a neck-to-neck race with Mark Spitz, when he hit the pool wall and ripped his stitches open! This hurt his timing, but Steve kept swimming and finished seconds behind Mark Spitz! Steve came home from the Olympics with a gold medal, a silver medal, and a bronze medal!

I've studied human beings and I can tell you that when they look beyond the obstacle to the reward, they'll forget the pain.

Again and again in your life you're going to have problems, setbacks, rejections, disappointments, discouragements, and prayers that seemingly are not answered. God may seem to be deaf. You may even think that prayer doesn't work and that God isn't real and Christ isn't real. You'll run into a stone wall. You'll hit bottom.

Keep on possibilitizing! Keep believing!

Possibilitizing Is Praying

"Play it down and pray it up." The sentence came into my mind, strong and forcefully—from God, I truly believe. I was flying from Korea to Sioux City, Iowa, to my daughter Carol's bedside, where I would have to face her for the first time since she had lost her leg. Facing me, sitting on the small fold-down seat, was a beautiful stewardess, elegant in her prim and polite uniform.

The seatbelt sign was still on. Her fingers were interlocked, her hands folded, resting on her knees. Suddenly, I noticed her *two* ankles, her *two* legs. Then I noticed the diamond ring and a wedding band on her left hand.

A horrible, negative thought came into my mind: *Would my*

*daughter, with a permanently severed limb, ever wear a diamond
ring? A wedding band?*

The tears overwhelmed me. Then came God's message loud
and clear, "Play it down and pray it up!" I believed He was
telling me, "I love your daughter; I have a plan for her life; I will
never stop loving her."

I cannot tell you how often since then with every passing year
I prayed for God to give Carol a love that would more than
compensate for whatever small part of her life she lost in that
surgical room in Sioux City, Iowa.

Eight years later, those prayers were answered when in her
wedding gown she walked elegantly down the aisle of the
Crystal Cathedral to become the wife of a tall, handsome, kind
man—Tim Milner—on March 29, 1986.

Possibilitizing Is Multiplying the Results

Are you tempted to quit because you don't see the returns
and the results? Sunday school teachers have quit at the Crystal
Cathedral because they didn't think they were doing a good job;
they couldn't see the results. Ministers have given up the
ministry because they thought they were failing. I know
salesmen who gave up because they thought they were bombing
out. If only these people had kept on possibilitizing and
mentally multiplying the possible results!

I am inspired by the story of George Smith, the Moravian,
who from his early years wanted to be a missionary. He finally
finished his preparation and traveled to Africa but was there
just a few months before being expelled. He left behind only
one convert, an old woman. He came back home and soon
died, still a young man, literally on his knees praying for Africa,
for the people he had come to love. Think of it! All of his life he
prepared—he went—he spent only a few months—he came

home and died. *But one hundred years later, that ministry to one old woman had blossomed into thirteen thousand happy Christians!*

Possibilitizing is multiplying what's going to happen!

Possibilitizing Is Overcoming While You're Undergoing

Colleen Johnson, my wife's executive secretary, knows what it is to overcome when you feel overwhelmed. Colleen is originally from Philadelphia. She married when she was only seventeen years old. She and her husband had a little girl when Colleen was nineteen. When her little girl was only two, Colleen's husband died suddenly at the age of twenty-five.

Then she found out that she was pregnant—a widow with a two-year-old and another child on the way. Colleen turned to her older brother, a seminary student, for support. They became close, but nine months later he had a heart attack and died. Colleen told me later, "At that point I realized the Lord was the one I must hold on to—He was the faithful one."

The years passed, and Colleen was married again to a great guy, Jimmy Johnson. He was a Christian and loved children. Together they left Philadelphia and came to California. A year later they started attending and then joined our drive-in church. They had a son, Mark. Then, two years later Glenn was born. He weighed only three pounds and had several problems. The most severe was that he had no rectal opening, a condition which required surgery the day he was born. Then Colleen and Jimmy learned their son was mentally retarded. But he lived through the surgery and became a very special boy. He had a great spirit. He loved everyone and was always ready to hug and kiss.

Then Jimmy was diagnosed with cancer. In 1977 he went through two surgeries and the cancer went into remission. But in 1979 the disease flared again in the liver. Jimmy died just before Christmas of that year.

We all shared Colleen's loss. Jimmy's smile had been infectious, and his face had lit up the choir loft every Sunday.

With the help of her older children, Colleen carried on, working full time and caring for Glenn. Even though his vocabulary was limited, his darling little face lighted up like no other! But Glenn missed his daddy terribly. He asked repeatedly, "Has Daddy gone to the doctor? The hospital? When is he coming home?" It was not easy for him to understand what it meant when they told him his daddy was gone. Colleen once found Glenn in her bedroom, sitting on the bed, looking at a picture of Jimmy that Glenn had taken on Thanksgiving Day. The picture, amazingly, had turned out nicely framed and focused—one of Colleen's favorites of her husband. Glenn talked and sang to the picture for almost fifteen minutes. This incident apparently settled his mind concerning Jimmy, for he no longer questioned his father's absence.

Not long after that, Glenn joined his daddy in heaven.

Somehow, in spite of all the difficulties that Colleen faced, she remained a woman of faith. She never stopped smiling. She never stopped working. She never stopped loving.

When I asked her how she did it, how she could keep on smiling, she said, "That's the way I feel. I know that everything is going to work out. I have Someone that I can hold onto. I always have, and I always will. And I'll always smile."

Possibilitizing Is Anticipating a Happy Ending

Are you tempted to turn back? Well, don't give up! *Don't quit when you're so close.* It would be a tragedy to come to the end of your life and have somebody say about you, "It's a pity he missed it. He quit just before he would have made it!"

We only have one chance to live this life. It would be a shame to throw away love and happiness because we're afraid that someday we'll lose the ones we love—afraid we'll get to the last page and discover a tragic ending.

What is a happy ending? Is it:

- "They lived happily ever after"?
- "They rode off into the sunset, two hearts intertwined forevermore"?

Listen to the following love story. Read it all the way to the end. Although at first you may not agree, it has, in my opinion, the happiest ending of all!

It happened years ago in a Midwest town. A wealthy man died leaving a rich and beautiful widow to mourn his passing. The pastor of their prestigious church was faithful in visiting the home to comfort the widow. He called the first week, then the second, and each week thereafter—month after month. His attention was deemed "unusual" by a few alert ladies of the town. Someone noticed that the shades were always drawn when he called at her home.

Rumors began to fly. Eyebrows were raised. A ruling elder was directed to look into the matter. The pastor's rounds were to be quietly and carefully monitored. On a given day he was seen driving up to her home. The elder was alerted by telephone. He headed for the pastor's study preparing to confront the reverend who, he was certain, would go from the widow's house to his private study in the church before he would go on to his own home and his wife in the manse.

An hour and more passed before the pastor opened his door and saw waiting for him a sober, serious, and suspicious elder. Even as the pastor entered he reeked with the rich fragrance of perfume!

The conversation was discreet but the elder's point was obvious—"You must stop calling on the widow, Reverend."

The pastor protested his innocence. Two weeks later the

Believe the best
about people!
And if
you're wrong,
you've only
made a
mistake
on
the side of love.

truth came out. The widow died! Now the pastor could tell the story. The woman had discovered that she had cancer just as her husband died. "When I'll need him most, on my road ahead, he will not be there! Pastor, help me!" she had pleaded. "Do not let me walk alone. And please, keep my illness a secret."

So each week the pastor had called—to pray, to comfort, to befriend.

"The light, it hurts my eyes, please draw the drapes." This had been her frequent request.

The last few weeks she had worn heavy perfumes to cover the unpleasant fragrances of medicines and the odors of her sickness.

The town gossips had believed the worst and were wrong! The pastor's wife always had believed the best about her husband and her best friend, the widow, and was right!

Love believes the *best*! So, when you are tempted to give up on love, to believe the worst, and to give in to suspicions, take the *high*-way to God's way of living! Have faith! Believe! You'll never be sorry you did!

THE ROAD OF LOVE:
Make It
Your-Way

Love! or Loneliness? You Decide!

"Love never ends."
     1 Corinthians 13:8

Now: It is time for *you* to take *action!*

Recipe: At best, this book is only a *recipe.* But a
                  recipe never fed anyone!

Blueprint: Hopefully, this book is a *blueprint* for
                  reconstructing human behavior and
                  human belief systems. But no blueprint
                  ever built anything!

Road Map: Surely, this book is a *road map*—but a road
                  map never took anyone anywhere.

Love, after all, is a choice. But consider the alternative:
Loneliness!

LONELINESS?

Many of you know her as "Dear Abby." Abigail Van Buren
said to me privately one day, "Dr. Schuller, loneliness, the need
for love, is the number one problem that faces people." We both
agreed that the deepest of all needs is to be accepted,
understood, yes, loved! The problem has not gone away. The
need has not lessened. We all still long for love. Many of us
suffer from the disease of loneliness.

Loneliness is caused by a battle between two persons who live inside of you. One person reaches out for love, like a little child in a candy store grasping for candy. This person desperately, anxiously, almost hysterically, longs for love and understanding. But another self, like a father holding back a child's hand in a candy store, says to your "grabbing" person, "Look out! Don't grab so fast. You might get hurt. You might be rejected. You don't want to love and be rejected, do you? Love is a risky business. To love is to be vulnerable. To be vulnerable is to be accountable. To be accountable is to run the risk of being rejected. Rejection is the risk of all risks: You might end up hating yourself because others don't love you!"

And so the lonely person is the one who ultimately listens to fear instead of to faith. The lonely person is the one who chooses the safe road, who listens finally to the self that says, "Be careful. Don't take any chances. Don't make any commitments. Don't get involved. You might get rejected. You might get hurt."

If that's the voice you listen to, if that's the road you choose, you will have your freedom intact, but the *price* you will pay for your freedom from involvement is *loneliness*.

One reason our society is so infected with loneliness is that the spirit of selfish freedom is so widespread. We don't want to risk losing our freedom by running the risks of making long-term commitments. So there are those who say, "What's the use of marriage? It's only a piece of paper. Live together; love together. Then if the relationship cools, you can split, you can go your way, and nobody will get hurt."

The fallacy of such a notion is that the man loves the woman only as long as she's young. Then when the wrinkles come, he deserts her. And when she's old, nobody cares.

We have a lot of lonely people today because unwillingness to make permanent commitments results in temporary interpersonal relationships. When people are hurt, they react like infantile children who pack up their marbles, go their way, and find themselves free once again. Those people will wake up one day and discover that nobody knows them and nobody cares!

Unless you are willing to surrender some freedom to make permanent commitments, you must be prepared to pay the price—*loneliness*!

Love dissolves loneliness, but love has a price tag, too. The price tag of love is commitment to continuity. As I said to a young couple the other day, "The one thing that makes marriage more important than a piece of paper, a license, is the commitment. Marriage says, 'I love you today and always will love you, even when our skin is wrinkled, even when the muscles sag, even when the hair thins.' Believe it or not, that's when you're going to need love more than ever."

WHERE ARE YOU?

If you've been afraid to make a commitment to love, if you've found that you are lost on the road of loneliness, if you would say to me if we met, "Dr. Schuller, I'm lost! I'm lonely! I want to get off!"—the first thing I'd ask you is, "Where are you? The road of loneliness has several paths. Before I can guide you or give you directions, I have to know where you're coming from."

Consider then the paths of loneliness; on which one are you?

The Loneliness of Sinking

The threat of failure, of course, brings its own type of loneliness! What is greater? The loneliness of success or the loneliness of failure? When things aren't going right and you're facing bankruptcy or your marriage is falling apart, you have that sinking, failing feeling; you are lonely because you don't want to share your failure with others. Nobody wants to hear a loser cry. Yet, precisely, here is where we need help and healing for our hurt.

Are you lonely in your sinking? Reach out! Open up! Be honest! After all, as I have said in *The Be Happy Attitudes*, "If you're too proud or too afraid to let people know you're hurting, don't be surprised if no one seems to care."

The Loneliness of Success

I don't know which is the worse. I have known both the loneliness of sinking and the loneliness of succeeding. There were two years in my ministry when my will to die was stronger than my will to live. I had dreams of a church with fountains and grounds where people could worship in their cars or inside the sanctuary. I had a vision for a tower with twenty-four-hour telephone counseling, a staff of great ministers, and a thousand volunteers who would do Christ's work. God had given me the whole dream. But the problems were momentous. Many times I thought the whole dream would dissolve. I was sure I was failing, but I couldn't get up in front of my church on Sunday morning and share my failures with my people. They had come for a lift themselves, and it was my responsibility to lift them, not lean on them. I felt the loneliness of *sinking*.

But I've also known the loneliness of *succeeding*. Think of it—when you succeed, who wants to listen to you? With whom can you share your victories? Most people will think you're boasting! So, in the wake of triumph, when everyone thinks you are on top and a great success, you may find yourself desperately lonely.

Are you lonely in your success?

Maybe you need to stop and remember that your success, if it is in your career, is nice—but it's really not all that wonderful in and by itself! After all, what is *real* success?

Real success is helping others, loving others, and being loved by them. *Real* success is building a family; it is sharing a smile or a meal; it is lending a hand. It is being interested in those around you who are real successes, too!

The Loneliness of Struggling

This path of loneliness is characterized by uncertainty; you don't know if you're sinking or succeeding. You do know you're struggling! You don't want to publicly admit you have problems or to show your weaknesses. You are reticent to display imperfection, so you strive to keep up a strong front. You don't want to expose the fact that you've got problems.

Are you lonely in your struggling?

First of all, it's important to acknowledge that every person in this world has problems. As Dr. Norman Vincent Peale once said in the Crystal Cathedral, "Everybody has problems. The only person who doesn't have problems is dead. Anybody who is really alive has problems."

I would add—anyone who is alive is someone who dares to get involved. A person who is getting involved is taking risks. And a person who is taking risks *will* have struggles! But isn't it better to be struggling and alive—a full-fledged member of the human race—than to be "dead" with boredom and loneliness?

The Loneliness of Striving

God gives you a dream. Should you tell people? There is the fear of what people will say, especially if you think big. Will they laugh and say, "Who do you think you are that you can be that person? Who do you think you are that you could amount to something? Boy, has something gone to your head! Wow, are you an egomaniac!" The fear of such ridicule drives many of us to strive *alone* to reach our dreams.

There is occasionally a legitimate fear that your ideas and your plans might be stolen by someone else. You may have to be protective of your concepts until you have an option, a copyright, or a patent. But isn't there usually at least one person you can trust who would love to hear your dream?

Are you lonely in your striving?

Perhaps you need to be reminded of the efforts of Dr. Howard House and Dr. William House. As I said in chapter seven, the House brothers developed the cochlear ear implant, which has been revolutionary in restoring hearing to children. Both of these men have impressed me with their willingness to share what they've learned with the medical community at large. They have not sought government aid for their work. It has all been private enterprise because their primary aim is to make their inventions and discoveries available to help as many people as possible. The Institute has no patents. I can assure you these men are far from lonely!

The Loneliness of Searching

Who has not known the loneliness of searching between two choices, searching for the best alternatives, searching for the right decision. In the final analysis, you *alone* make most of the decisions in your life. No one can make them for you. This part of your life will always be separate from the part of your life that interacts with others.

Most of us live in interpersonal relationships, acting and reacting to the challenges, instincts, and impulses of the people around us.

There is another part of your life that you live totally alone. You were born alone. Even if you are a twin, both of you were born individually—alone. When you learned to walk, you learned to walk alone. When you learned to talk, you learned to talk alone. True, there were those who guided, supported, and sustained you. But *you* did it—*alone!*

When you must make the great decisions—your career or profession or whom you will marry—you make them alone! Your father doesn't make them, your mother doesn't make them, your friends don't make them. You do! Others may advise and attempt to persuade or dissuade, but in the final analysis, you must search through the discussions, arguments, reasons, pros and cons and decide!

Are you lonely in your searching?

Why not consider meeting my good friend, Jesus Christ. He will walk with you in your times of *searching* . . . as well as in your time of separation.

The Loneliness of Separation

For all of us there comes the time when we will die. That is another moment that you will go through alone. There will be those who will stand by you. They will be supportive and helpful, but you will die alone. All alone. *Unless* you have a very special friend.

A few years ago, I sat at the bedside of a lovely woman. She had cancer and had taken every form of chemotherapy and radiation treatment. But after all this, the doctors told her that she only had a short time to live.

I sat by her side, held her hand, and repeated to her the words my mother found so helpful on her deathbed:

"Fear not, for I have redeemed you;
I have called you by your name;
You are Mine.
When you pass through the waters,
I will be with you;
And through the rivers, they shall not overflow you.
When you walk through the fire, you shall not be burned,
Nor shall the flame scorch you.
For I am the LORD, your God." (Isa. 43:1–3)

Are you lonely in your separations?

The river, the fire, the flame of separations—of losing loved ones, whether through death or divorce—need not consume you. You will not be overwhelmed if you have the Lord, your God, to *lead* you through! To *walk* you through! To *carry* you through!

The Loneliness of Sinning

No failure is more depressing than moral failure! It defies calculation—how much loneliness and alienation is related to secret sins harbored in human hearts. Who dares to expose their hidden shortcomings? Who is not naturally inclined to cover up and conceal their private iniquities? What stress does this loneliness place on our emotional system? And what is our salvation? Is there a safe release? Can confession liberate us from the bondage of guilty isolation?

"No" and "Yes." "No"—confession is destructive if it exposes our worst self to persons who could use it against us. "Yes"—if confession is made humbly, honestly, and hopefully to someone who loves us totally, trustfully! That Person to me is Jesus Christ! That's why I call Him Savior!

LOVE OR LONELINESS? YOU DECIDE!

Wherever you are on the road of life, even if it be on any of the paths of loneliness, you can choose, you can decide where it is you want to go. Your final destination is in your hands. So stop! Quit blaming your loneliness on:

- Parents
- Ex-spouses
- Hurtful, deceitful lovers
- Critical teachers
- Harsh employers
- Two-faced "friends"
- Cold, isolated society

Instead, start! Begin to believe in *love!*

It's true that loneliness permeates our world. But so does love! We only need to choose which we want to look for, which we want to have.

You can choose to be lonely, or you can choose to love and be loved! It all starts when you choose to accept God's love for you.

ANYBODY CAN FIND LOVE!

The late Corrie ten Boom inspired me with a thought years ago: "No problem is too big for God's power; no person is too small for God's love."

One day, when two of our girls were quite young, Mrs. Schuller and I took them to our cabin high in the California mountains. Gretchen, our youngest, came to me one morning and said, "Daddy, in our Bible school our teacher said that if you take a pine cone and put peanut butter on it and you sprinkle it with birdseed, the birdseed will stick to the pine cone, and you can hang it in a tree for the birds to eat."

"You don't have to go through all that," I answered. "We've got some birdseed here in the cabin. Just put it out on the deck. The birds will come and eat it."

She did as I suggested. She sprinkled the birdseed along the railing of the deck, and sure enough, the blue jays came and gobbled it up. Next the squirrels came, chased the blue jays away, and finished every crumb of birdseed.

"I still think I should put the seed on a pine cone with peanut butter," my daughter persisted. It sounded like a nice project, so I agreed to help her.

We went for a walk in the woods, and under one of the great old trees in the forest we found some pine cones and took them home. I tied a rope to the very top prong of the cone so that I could hang it from a branch of a tree. Then we got out the peanut butter. It was a mess trying to spread peanut butter all over the wood scales of the pine cone.

Then Gretchen sprinkled the birdseed on, and sure enough, it all stuck to the peanut butter. We took it outside and hung it on a branch, right on the tip so it hung down, drooping on the branch like a too-heavy ornament on the tender tip of a Christmas tree.

"Gretchen," I said, "you should tie it in the middle of the branch, where the branch is stronger."

"No," she said, "I'll tie it here at the end."

So she left it hanging there on the end. Pretty soon the blue jays came, but they just flew around and didn't dare to land on the pine cone, because it was weaving back and forth and looked too unsteady for them. They didn't dare to sit on it. They stood on the branch, but when they couldn't begin to get at the cone beneath them, they flew away in disgust.

Pretty soon the squirrels came. They had smelled the peanut butter. Up the tree they went and onto the branch. I can still see one of them running down the branch until it started to bend, then backing off fearfully and running back down the trunk of the tree. What a lesson in frustration! He went back up another branch, trying to approach it from another direction, but he never got within two feet. Finally, he ran off.

"Gretchen," I said, "it's a sublime failure. They can't eat it." And then something wonderful happened. All the *little* birds started coming. They came and literally walked down the rope and nibbled the food from the top so they wouldn't get their feet dirty with the peanut butter. It was an amazing sight! Then more little birds came. One very resourceful, "possiblity thinking" winged creature grabbed the bottom of the pine cone where there was no peanut butter with his feet and ate from the bottom. So, the *little* birds had their feast. And the big blue jay and the squirrel were unable to take the food from the little ones.

This illustrates the good news I have for you! As far as the food for your heart is concerned, God has set things up in such a way that the lonely people can always get what they need, the love their hearts hunger for! *Anybody* can find the road of love.

Love is not a chance! It is a choice!

Love is not luck! It is an election!

Love is not a result of fate! It is a result of faith!

Love is not a result of luck, environment, or genetics. It is the result of a decision! You mistakenly may have assumed that the people who find someone to love them are the lucky ones. Or they're the ones who were raised in a family environment that stimulated love. Or they are the people who were born with loveable personalities.

This is a myth! Don't let it keep you from finding love for yourself, for the truth is that love *is* a choice! It is an act of faith. It is a cognitive decision to believe in others, to believe in yourself, and to believe in the love of God.

ACCEPT THE LOVE THAT ENDS ALL LONELINESS!

You can travel around the world and meet Christians in every country. And when you talk to them about their faith, the conversation will quickly focus on the life and person of someone named Jesus of Nazareth, who lived two thousand years ago. When you ask them what Jesus means to them, you will get many different answers because Christians have different concepts of Jesus Christ. But if you will listen at a deeper level, you will conclude that they all agree about one thing: *Christ is Love!*

A remarkable unique quality of Christ's life was that He was *Love Incarnate*. And that makes the difference! No other religious leader claimed to have the authority from heaven to forgive sins. And the scars in His palms give him enormous credibility! He had love! He lived it! He died because of love! And He rose again in love! This quality of love makes all the difference in the world! And I want to help you to see that if you choose to put Christ's love at the central core of your life, a rising power within you will change everything!

If you "by *chance*" encounter love, you might question if it is real love. But if you encounter somebody who has *chosen* to love, then you will have found *real* love, a love that ends all loneliness!

It matters not who you are, where you are coming from, or where you have been. If you are a mother, a business person, a teacher, a lawyer, a criminal, or a prostitute, you can find real love! It doesn't require wealth, or education, or connections with powerful people. It doesn't require talent, intelligence, or even beauty to be loved. It only requires choosing to believe and accept the fact that God loves you—just the way you are!

I met her in Hawaii. I shall never forget her, for she became for me the symbol of hurt, despair, and loneliness. I was in Hawaii resting and being renewed after the busy Christmas season at the Crystal Cathedral. I love to walk a particular beautiful, unpopulated beach there. The white sand is dotted with graceful coconut palms; the tropical breezes caress my skin with their balmy warmth. The sun's hot rays seem to draw all tension from me. Time on this beach is very therapeutic for me.

One day while walking this beach, I carried with me a copy of a previous book of mine, *Tough Minded Faith for Tender Hearted People,* and a notebook in which I could jot down my thoughts. I walked to the rocks, as I often do, for I am seldom recognized or interrupted there.

I enjoyed a wonderful time of meditation, reading, and writing, and then I waded through the shallow, gently rippling surf on my way back to my room. Two women were wading in the water about twenty feet away.

Suddenly, one of them called out, "Are you on television?"
I said that I was.
Coming closer, she asked, "Are you an actor?"
"No. I give speeches."

"What do you speak about?"

I motioned to the books I was holding in my hand and said, "I speak about the same stuff as I write about. I write books."

"What are you writing a book about?"

I noticed that this young woman had a tattoo on her shoulder and her eyes were empty. "I'm writing a book entitled, *Be Happy—You Are Loved!*"

"What does that mean?"

"That means that happiness in life is not based on the money you earn or the clothes you wear; it matters not where you live or what you do; it matters not what happens to you. Even if you've experienced tragedy or triumph, you *can* be happy for one reason—you are loved!"

She gave me a skeptical look at that point, so I quickly continued, "Every person has value. Every person has worth."

She looked down at the sand. I could tell she didn't believe a word I was saying. Suddenly, I had an idea; I think it was heaven-sent. I said, "Say, you know I often interview people for my books. Could I interview you?"

"Well, I guess that would be O.K."

I started off with what I thought was a safe question: "What do you do?"

She just looked at me. When she failed to answer my question, I asked, "Don't you have a job? Don't tell me you are retired at such a young age?"

"No," she replied, "but what I do, people don't normally talk about."

"What could that be?"

She hesitated and then said, "Do you really write books?"

I turned the copy of my book over and showed her my picture on the back.

She didn't bat an eye. She said, "I am a prostitute."

Whatever answer I had expected—it surely wasn't this.

She hastened to add, "I am not a street girl. I am a call girl."

I decided to continue the interview for I truly wondered how a girl could end up like this. Here is the story as she told it to me:

She was twenty-eight years old, white, born and raised in Atlanta, Georgia. There she got her RN degree, married, and had a baby. She and her husband divorced, so she went to Honolulu to find a new life. As she explained it to me, she and her girlfriends went to bed with guys anyway, so why not charge them for it?

"Are you proud of your work?" I asked.

Not prepared for her answer, I was shocked when she said, "Yes, I am proud of it. I'm the best. I earn the most money."

I challenged her claim by asking, "How do you know? Do you report it to the government?"

"No."

"Do you know what the other girls get?"

"No."

"So if you are not ashamed of what you do, then why don't you brag about it?"

Her silence was as close to an admission that I would get that deep down she had some feelings of shame that she would not admit to herself, much less to a stranger.

The next question I asked was, "What about morality? Does that enter in?"

"I don't think I am doing anything immoral. The people who are killing are immoral. I don't kill people."

"Next question: What about religion? Do you have any?"

"No."

"Have you ever been to any kind of synagogue, church, or temple in your life?"

"Yes. Twice. Sunday school in Atlanta."

"Another subject: Jesus Christ. What do you know about Him?" I shall never forget her answer. I still almost tremble at it.

"Jesus Christ . . . I think He lived and died, didn't He?" she said.

"Is that all you know about Him?"

"That's all I know."

I was stunned! Shocked! Here stood a young woman who only two years earlier had been a nurse, married, the mother of a baby in Atlanta, Georgia. Today she was a call girl in Honolulu, and all she knew was that Jesus was someone who "lived and died, didn't He?"

Before I left she said, "I would like to read one of your books."

I gave her the one that I was holding. "My name is Robert Schuller. I'm on television. Read the book. Watch me on TV. I think you might just love what I say, because I will tell you more about Jesus Christ."

By now her whole manner had changed. Her cold, tough shell seemed to melt. An openness, an attractive humility, an appealing vulnerability seemed to take over. I added, "And you just might discover for the first time in your life what love really is."

She took the book and said, "Thank you. Maybe I'll see you again someday."

I pray every day that she will read and she will watch and she will listen and she will open her heart to the One who will teach her about love. It would be my greatest joy to meet her again some day, to hear her say, "Remember me? I'm the call girl you interviewed. I have found Jesus! I have found real love for the first time in my life!"

In the meantime I will be haunted by her description of Jesus Christ as someone who "lived and died, didn't He?"

Jesus Christ was much more than just a man who lived and died. He was much more than just a prophet. He was God come to earth as a man to die on a cross to tell us how very much God loves us.

Dr. William Glasser, whose book *Reality Therapy* has been

helpful to many people, has a sentence that I find very, very significant: "Every [person] needs one essential friend." I would add: If you've got that, then you've got a cure for loneliness.

Each one of us should have one friend so intimate that we can expose ourselves completely without fear of rejection, without fear we will be shamed! Without fear that someday we'll be exposed! Where can you find a friend you can trust like that? I have such a friend. His name is Jesus Christ. He is that one essential friend.

You will never get lonely as long as there is one person who loves you with a love so great that you know you don't have to be a phony around Him. You don't have to play games. You don't have to wear a mask. You don't have to pretend. He loves you anyway. He will never condemn you. He will never scold you. He will never belittle you.

I can go to Him and confess all my sins—of thought, word, and deed—and know that He will put His arms around my shoulder and love me anyway:

- I can go to Him in the Loneliness of Striving—He will *encourage* me!
- I can go to Him in the Loneliness of Searching for Alternatives—He will *guide* me!
- I can go to Him in the Loneliness of Struggling and Sinking—He will *support* me!
- I can go to Him in the Loneliness of Succeeding—He will *rejoice* with me!
- I can go to Him in the Loneliness of Sinning—He will *save* me!

Well, then—Love or Loneliness?—it's your choice! The secret of happiness is so simple: Become a "God loves you . . . and so do I" person! Accept Jesus Christ as your Savior and best Friend. Become a "one-to-One-for-someone" person.

Now let me give you a final blessing—this prayer:

May the Lord
touch your heart
with his finger
of love and leave a fingerprint
no one can rub off. Robert Schuller